JOEY HULIN

Retreat YOURSELF

HOW TO CREATE A
TRULY TRANSFORMATIVE
SELF-LED RETREAT

VERBENA

Contents

Chapter One

Introduction

A retreat of any kind is a journey. It is a transition from everyday life – a life of outward pursuits and of giving, giving, giving or doing, doing, doing – into a quiet space of mind-body-soul nourishment, introspection and being. A self-led retreat is a pilgrimage inward, designed by you, for you. A self-led retreat isn't a boot camp for self-reliance or ultra independence, but quite the opposite: it is an accessible, affordable means of taking responsibility for your own wellbeing. It is an ultimate act of self-care, empowering you to self-lead in your own health, healing and self-discovery journey.

This book will guide you through the journey and step-by-step process of creating your own self-led retreat. It will offer you the guidance, inspiration, support and tools you need to design yourself a truly transformative retreat experience, before encouraging you to give yourself permission to dive in, and immerse yourself completely in the magical, mystical world of retreats.

Retreat magic

Immersed among ancient oak trees, sat on the banks of the river Fal in Cornwall, England, I felt a grounded sense of aliveness in my heart. A steady balance of peace, of joy, acceptance and hope. I felt rested yet energised, open yet contained. I felt a deep sense of ease and peace within my own being. "This is the magic of retreats", I thought to myself.

Retreat offerings have bloomed in recent years, perhaps as an antidote to the epidemic of stress and busyness the modern world has swept us along in. Retreats offer us a held space for quiet, nourishment and self-reflection. In a world that says "You need to do more", a retreat will soothe us by saying "Do less". Where the modern world wants to keep us distracted by algorithms, wanting more and striving to be more, retreats offer a space to slow down, and reconnect with the natural world and what really matters. In a world so geared toward the extroverted, retreats and especially self-led retreats offer gentle souls a safe place to realign and top up their energy

The difference between a retreat and a holiday (vacation) is subtle on the surface, but ocean deep underneath. A retreat embroils self-discovery, looking inward and taking conscious, deliberate rest. Attending a retreat is often driven by a desire for healing or self-connection, or to feel recharged or gain a deeper sense of mental or emotional clarity. A holiday, on the other hand, is more focused on external discovery such as sightseeing or exploring different cultures, or having some much-needed, light-hearted fun.

There is a time and place for both. But retreats allow us to lovingly tend to ourselves in a held space, and are what I consider to be an ultimate act of self-care. They can act as a reset button, helping us shift gears into a deeper, slower and more authentic way of living. Deciding to go on a self-led retreat can be an incredibly empowering experience, so I am excited that you are here. Leading yourself in this way is the embodiment of divine feminine energy.

Attending any retreat starts with an intention and a conscious choice to carve out sacred time to step off the treadmill of daily life and disengage from distractions. In some ways, the decision to retreat requires courage, as you choose to turn your awareness inward and not hide from yourself. The choice to book onto an organised group retreat – an experience that often comes with a pretty hefty price tag – instead of a holiday says something about where we are in life, who we are and what we value. I've been running wellness retreats since 2015 and I find it interesting that those who book onto a retreat all seem to have a similar sort of something about them. I've found that retreats often attract people – mostly women – who are of different ages and have different backgrounds, experiences and personalities, but are much the same in spirit. A retreat is a meeting of like-minded souls who seem to see the world in a similar way, and it all starts with an intention.

An intention is the seed that must be planted and nurtured in order for the blossoming, thriving tree to grow. An intention lines up the starting blocks in the direction we wish to travel. It is a potent yet utterly simple way of empowering ourselves in the present moment, and it has the ability to make the mundane sacred, to turn daily life into a prayer and to transform otherwise ordinary time and space into a retreat experience.

My journey of retreats

Back in 2015, I knew I was in desperate need of a retreat, but there were limited retreats on offer. It seemed that many of the retreats available were the super spiritual, serious retreats that were heavily focused on following an approach or method, or on one specific school of thought or philosophy. There were also retreats at the other end of the spectrum, such as super light-hearted yoga holidays with no real depth to them other than a class in the morning and evening. I was aching for a warm, welcoming experience that didn't take itself too seriously, but that had some depth to it: something that offered a lovingly held space and non-judgemental guidance that would help me reconnect to myself and to nature. I wanted nourishing activities, but I also wanted plenty of room in the schedule to reflect and just be.

Years previous to this, I had moved through burnout, and my first experience of a "dark night of the soul" – an expereince where I questioned and re-evaualted all I thought I knew about life and myself. Emerging slowly, I felt as if I was standing at the edge of a thick fog in my life. I could see and feel the light on the horizon in the distance, but I had no idea how to get there. I knew the only way to reach the other side would be to enter the fog – the unknown – and to place one foot in front of the other and trust in the path as it was unfolding. Fast forward to 2015 – and my desire to attend a retreat I could not find – and I decided to create the retreat experience I was in need of as an offering for others. I called these retreat offerings Horizon Inspired.

Nearly a decade and 80 retreats later, I have learnt a lot about retreat experiences. One thing I know for certain is that for most people, there is a certain magic that happens during a retreat. Most people emerge having received exactly what they needed, even those who came to the retreat not knowing what it was that drew them there or what they needed. It became obvious to me very early on that any insights or feelings of alignment and empowerment experienced during a retreat was owned fully by the retreat attendees themselves; it was their ability to enter the experience and really be a part of it. The venue, teachers, schedule, teachings and food helped, but none of these things were the magic ingredient that sparked the difference between having a lovely time or having a life-changing time. That bit was 100 per cent owned by them, and is something they took away with them.

Since 2015, the retreat industry – or wellness tourism as it is sometimes referred to – has boomed. There are retreats of all different shapes and sizes, catering for just about any interest or need. Industry data is showing a significant increase in demand for retreats since the Covid-19 pandemic. A National Geographic article dedicated to this phenomenon reports a 30 per cent increase in demand for wellness breaks between 2021 and 2022, and found that almost half (46 per cent) of global travellers are more open to wellness breaks than ever before. Now you can find creative retreats, dance retreats, singing retreats, plant medicine retreats and everything else in between.

I truly believe in the power of retreats, and it fills me with joy that no matter who you are and what you need, you should be able to find an experience that suits your needs and interests. There is just one (quite significant) problem: you have to have a decent amount of disposable income in order to attend one.

Group retreats are expensive for both the guest and the host. I know the price I have to charge in order to make a retreat viable is not affordable for most people, and it has always sat uncomfortably with me. I also lived the irony where I was running multiple retreats a year, yet couldn't afford to attend one myself. In fact, it was being in this position that first led me to the unexpected power of a self-led solo retreat.

Self-led retreats

The first time I took myself on a self-led solo retreat, it was largely spurred on by the deep desire and need for a retreat – a need to get away and clear my head – and a lack of funds to join an organised group one. I had no expectation that it would be remotely as beneficial as a group retreat. I just knew I needed to retreat and get away.

I booked two nights in a friend's holiday cottage not far from home, and decided that in order to make the most of my time there, I would design a retreat schedule and get super prepared, just as I would when holding space for other people. I didn't want to have to get in my car or engage in the outside world for the whole two days.

I set the intention to completely hand myself over fully to the experience from the moment I arrived. Emerging on the other side, I was surprised to find I felt all the benefits I was hoping to feel, and that I had experienced the same sort of magic as I did from a group retreat. It cemented a thought I'd had since I ran my very first retreat: the true magic of a retreat doesn't lie in the location, the leader or the group, but in our own individual intention and ability to hand ourselves over fully to the experience. To self-lead. Any insights, wisdom or inner shifts that are experienced while on retreat – group or self-led – are all owned by and because of you.

Handing yourself over to the experience means being fully present to it, unshackling yourself from preconceived expectations for it to be a certain way, and instead opening yourself up to what is and to whatever will unfold. It means to stay present in the experience and to bring a beginner's mind and a willing heart to it from start to finish. It requires an element of surrender, handing over control and yielding to be held or guided by the experience itself.

Solo retreats are nothing new. The history of them is rich, but usually a little on the extreme side, such as vision quests or pilgrimages. A vision quest is usually time spent in the wilderness, alone, with no access to food, water or sleeping arrangements. Just like all types of retreats, there is a time and place for this sort of retreat, but they can be quite masculine in nature. The self-led retreats we are exploring and designing in this book, on the other hand, offer a deeply feminine, nourishing and restorative alternative to other solo retreats. Where vision quests are about discomfort and abstinence, our self-led retreat will involve comfort and feeling held.

A retreat – whether it's group or self-led – is the deliberate carving out of time and space to pause. The activities are a vehicle for reconnection, and the carved-out space for self-reflection is where the true and lasting magic happens. While for a lot of people, the bonds formed with others on group retreats can be one of the highlights, for some, navigating group dynamics and different energies can be distracting and, at times, challenging. A self-led retreat is designed specifically to meet all of your own individual needs, allowing you to connect with yourself on a profoundly deep level.

Creating your own retreat experience at home, or in holiday accommodation to your liking and budget, is the ultimate act of self-care. When done right, I have found that a self-led retreat can be just as powerful as a group experience.

Self-led retreats have become an annual occurrence for me. My self-led retreats usually involve two nights (sometimes more) at a cheap holiday let where I take myself off to reconnect. I put just as much time and energy into lovingly designing and curating these experiences as I do with the group retreats I organise for other people. I plan a menu and prepare delicious, nutritious foods, snacks and drinks (including all of my favourite things). I have a good idea of what activities I'd like to include, but allow for flexibility too. I make sure I turn my phone off for the duration of the retreat. And most importantly of all, I set an intention. I make that intention clear, memorable and achievable, and I always leave feeling topped up, clear, calm, grounded and excited about the life I'm going back to, and the changes I am going to make. Stumbling across the power of self-led retreats excited me because it showed me that there is a solution to the issue of the growing affordability gap, and that it can be closed without loss of quality or depth of experience.

How to use this book

In this spirited, easy-to-use guide, I will offer you guidance on how to plan, design and prepare for your own self-led retreat. Among these pages, you will find a pick and mix of retreat activities, rituals, readings and more, all offered to support you in your preparation for and experience of your self-led retreat.

A self-led retreat is a truly empowering experience. Your retreat will be designed and led by you, at a budget that works for you. Whether it's one night away in a cheap holiday let or a 5* hotel in your local town, or an afternoon home-based activity, it has the power to be just what you need if you hand yourself over fully to the experience.

This book has been designed to be worked through systematically, so grab a journal that you can dedicate specifically to this self-led retreat experience, and work your way through the book chapter by chapter.

First, in Chapter Two: Planning your retreat, you will be coached through the planning stages of your retreat to get crystal clear on what it is you truly need, and the tools and resources you might need access to to bring your retreat to life. Next, in Chapter Three: Curating your retreat activities, you will be offered a pick and mix menu of practices and activities to choose from for your retreat. Moving on to Chapter Four: Your retreat, you will be offered support and guidance for the first day of your retreat. This chapter also includes support for you as you move through the retreat itself, and advice for staying focused and navigating any resistance should it surface. And finally, in Chapter Five: Integration, you will find guidance on how to integrate your learnings and reflections into your daily life.

I hope this guide inspires you to take some sacred time for yourself. I hope it acts as a trusted companion as you embark on your own self-led retreat. And I hope it feels like something you can turn to as a trusted friend and companion whenever you feel the need to reconnect.

Are you ready to prioritise you and start planning your self-led retreat? Let's do this!

DATE
I am excited about
Most important task of the day

Chapter Two

Planning your retreat

Welcome to the planning stage of your retreat. Here, you will put on the hat as retreat organiser, much like you would if you were planning on hosting a retreat for paying guests. As a professional retreat host and a self-led retreat enthusiast, I know this is a vital step in the process that cannot be rushed or overlooked. So in this chapter, we will explore the power of intention and the importance of space and setting.

Let this planning stage be an act of self-care in itself. If you can, carve out half an hour here and there to work through this section. In it, you will be guided to explore what it is you are truly in need of; the tools you will need to nourish yourself with; and the all-important part of booking a date and a venue for your retreat. First, let's get clear on what it is that you truly need right now so that this can shape your intention and your self-led retreat.

What do I need most?

It is a beautiful, simple self-care practice to at least once a day – no matter how busy or stressed you are – place your hand on your heart, take a deep inhale and ask yourself: what do I most need right now? Sometimes, an intuitive answer comes flooding forth. At other times, the answer is so buried beneath the surface that it is hard to translate what your heart is yearning for.

To uncover what you need most right now, I invite you to practise the following short meditation, which will help you drop from your head to your heart before journalling your thoughts and feelings. This exercise will also give you a good idea of what you will be working with during your self-led retreat.

The meditation

Follow these simple steps, or, to hear a guided recording of this meditation, scan this QR code. You will need: a quiet place; your new journal; and two different coloured pens.

- Start by taking a few breaths to centre yourself. Bring your consciousness awareness to the sensations of each breath, and feel a sense of grounding and settling with the out-breath. After three deep breaths, allow your breath to find its natural rhythm.
- Notice if you're gripping any muscles in your body by scanning your whole body, paying particular attention to any areas you know you carry stress, like your shoulders, jaw, the space between your eyebrows or your belly. Consciously soften and relax all your muscles.
- Take your awareness to your heart space and imagine every breath clearing out any energetic tension or tightness around your heart. I like to imagine a light in the centre of my heart, like a flame that grows brighter and stronger with every conscious breath. Spend a few moments connecting with that light and energy in your heart.
- Place one or both hands over your heart and ask yourself the question: what do I need most? Allow time for an intuitive response to come.
- Close the meditation by taking a final, long inhale before opening your eyes.

The reflection

- Next, pick up your journal and pen and jot down or sketch out what came to you during the meditation. This might be a short phrase like "To rest" or "To find joy", or it might be something more descriptive like "To be kinder to myself" or "To start making healthier choices for myself". Write your phrase out clearly on the page.
- Start exploring why this phrase has appeared on the page. Write about why you think it is on the page, avoiding the temptation to edit your answer. Your answer might look like "Because I've been so busy lately looking after everyone else".
- Once you feel as if you have answered yourself, dig in deeper and ask "Why?" again. Your answer might look like "Because people need me to be there for them and I struggle to make time for myself".
- Keep asking "Why?", digging deeper to uncover the "Why?" at the root of it all.

To close

- Skim-read through your answers and, in a different coloured pen, circle the needs that you are seeing surface. This might look like "I need to be heard" or "I need to take better care of myself".
- Place your hands over your heart, close your eyes, take a deep breath and whisper "Thank you".

The power of intention

Now that you have a clearer idea of your needs right now, it's time to set an intention for your self-led retreat. This will offer you an anchor point from which to tether yourself to so that you can get the most out of the experience.

In simple terms, an intention is a consciously chosen thought or set of thoughts that helps us experience a desired result. So much power is held in intention. An intention isn't a goal, or something you can tick off a list or a destination to be reached. An intention isn't rigid either. Instead, an intention offers us a tool for embodying a way of being and guides our choices and behaviours in the direction we wish our lives and experiences to go in, while leaving plenty of room for surprises. When we set intentions, we know that ultimately, we are not in control, but that we do have agency over how we show up in our experiences and in the choices we make for ourselves. At times when we feel lost or overwhelmed, pausing to set an intention can act as a torch that illuminates the path ahead, and helps us to feel more steady and sure-footed.

Once you are clear on what you need from your self-led retreat – which will essentially drive your motivation to plan one – you can set an intention for your experience. This intention will form an anchor that you will stay tethered to, and that will keep you on track.

Setting an intention

Scan over and reflect on your musings from your meditation in "What do I need most?" from earlier in this chapter. Does a pattern or a theme emerge? What are you feeling as you reflect and feel into your needs right now? Can these insights be turned into an intention? This might be something like "To slow down", "To focus on myself for a change", "To get clear on what I want", "To recharge" or "To remember who I am".

Once you have an intention, write it out clearly in big, bold, beautiful and colourful letters in your journal. You will come back to this in Chapter Four: Your retreat, when you're setting up for your retreat.

Booking your retreat

A retreat is often described as a quiet or secluded place in which one can rest and relax, or a period or place of seclusion for the purposes of prayer and meditation. So it's unsurprising that space and setting are crucial to creating a special retreat experience.

If you have ever booked a group retreat, you might have selected that specific experience because of the venue or location. But a self-led retreat setting can be anything to suit your preference and budget. Perhaps you like the sound of a remote cabin in the woods. Perhaps you are enticed by a country house hotel with a spa. Perhaps your budget will allow one night away somewhere. Or maybe you'd prefer to stay at home. You are the organiser, so you get to decide. Get clear on the budget you have to work with, and do some research to cost-up what you are able to or would like to book.

If you can't afford your ideal venue this time, consider how you could bring elements of it into your retreat experience. For example, if you'd love to book a cabin in the woods but will be holding your self-led retreat at home due to a tight budget, is there a local forest where you could spend some time during the retreat? Or might camping be an option?

Once you have an idea of where you'd like your retreat to take place, secure a date. Run this date past anyone you need to first. Then, before you click "Book", reconnect with your heart and your intention. See the act of booking this self-led retreat as a powerful act of self-care in and of itself. Then, consciously book it.

Questions to ask yourself or get clear on:

- What is your budget?
- What would your ideal location and venue be and why?
- What facilities or resources would you like access to? The ocean, a spa, wild open spaces, lake view, woods, cosy rural vibes?
- How do these align with what you need most right now?

Preparing your tool kit

Once you have a date and venue booked, it's time to plan the tools you might need to bring with you to have the best experience. Engaging your five senses during your retreat can help you stay present and connected to your intention, and create a sense of a retreat experience. Yoga teachers who take time to set up a space beautifully can transform a simple village hall and one-hour yoga class into a delicious, spa-like experience with the use of smells, lighting and sounds. This is something that you too can do for your self-led retreat, which requires just a little pre-thought and planning.

You want to arrive at your experience with all you will need so that you can really immerse yourself in the experience itself (and not have to visit the shops to pick up candles mid-retreat). If you have decided to stay at home, there are plenty of ways you can prepare your space for a retreat, and transform it into a retreat setting. These include: ensuring your space has been cleared of clutter and is tidy and fresh; deciding on which rooms you will mainly use (you might create a yoga space in the spare bedroom, for example); and asking yourself: what do I need to do to create a sacred space for my self-led retreat?

The most important thing to do wherever you are is turn off your TV. You might like to find a pretty blanket or throw ahead of your retreat to place over the TV to cover it, whether this is in a hotel room or at home. A retreat is a sacred opportunity to reconnect with yourself, and digital distractions of all kinds are just that: a distraction.

Here is a list of a few of my favourite tools that you might like to include in your self-led retreat tool kit. Planning these ahead of time allows you to purchase or borrow items before your retreat starts so you can arrive fully prepared.

Aura/room cleansing spray – This can be used as an alternative to burning smoke to spiritually cleanse a space, making it more appropriate for hotel rooms or venues away from home. These are pre-prepared bottles of essential oil and water blends, and are sometimes blessed or infused with Reiki. A quick online search will provide you with plenty of options, or you might choose to make your own.

Bolsters, cushions and blocks – Bolsters and blocks are frequently used in yin yoga and other relaxation practices, and can sometimes be hired or borrowed from your local yoga studio or teacher. If you don't have access to them, arm yourself with lots of cushions for your retreat. These can be used in restorative postures indoors and for relaxing outside.

Books – Bringing carefully selected texts with you is advised, alongside any books you are reading at the moment for pure enjoyment. This might be a book of poetry, a sacred text or books you know help you reconnect to yourself or your sense of spirituality on a deeper level.

Candles – Candles are an essential in your "retreat yourself" tool kit. Lighting a candle for any activity – especially meditation – is such a powerful way of setting an intention for the practice and remaining focused. I often light a candle before I start writing and blow it out when I'm done. This can also be done for a journalling practice, yoga practice or meditation. Having candles safely burning just creates such a dreamy, relaxing, retreat-like environment.

Chimes, singing bowls, tuning forks, gongs – Using carefully tuned instruments like crystal bowls, chimes or gongs is a powerful aid to meditation, but are often a bit pricey to purchase. You might be able to borrow or rent an instrument for your retreat from a local yoga studio, teacher or holistic therapist.

Clothing – Many people come to group retreats having bought themselves a new pair of yoga leggings or pjs especially for it, but this is often driven by the fact that other people will see them in them, rather than as an act of self-care to honour themselves. You might wish to buy yourself something new as a treat, and if so, do it for you. Bringing clothing that is comfortable and practical is also essential on any retreat. Pack your dressing gown if you're not staying in a hotel that provides one.

Crystals – You might like to do a little bit of research to find a crystal or crystals that match your retreat intention. Small tumblestones are inexpensive and can be found online or in New Age stores for very little money. For inspiration, three good all rounders and favourites of mine are: black tourmaline, rose quartz and citrine. Black tourmaline is great for grounding; citrine is used for boosting mood and positive energy; and rose quartz is a calming, balanced stone that emits a vibration of love.

Essential oils – Aromatherapy is a powerful tool with a wide range of uses. Natural essential oils can help induce relaxation and clarity, boost mood and aid concentration. There are over 90 types of essential oils, so spend a little time doing some research or consulting with an aromatherapist to find the right ones for you. You can diffuse oils in a diffuser, burn them in an oil burner, apply them (diluted) to your pulse points or put drops of skin-safe varieties into a bath for bathing. There are lots of companies that offer delicious blends of oils. Just check that any essential oil you buy is 100 per cent pure to ensure you are working with the best quality oil. Three recommended essential oils to include in your retreat bag are: lavender for relaxation; peppermint for focus; and eucalyptus for clarity.

Fairy lights – If you are planning on taking your retreat in a hotel, bringing a set of fairy lights or battery-powered tea lights or candles are a good alternative to open-flame candles, as they create a magical, relaxing atmosphere.

Flowers – Buying yourself flowers is such a beautiful act of self-care at any time and, in my opinion, is an essential self-care tool to delight the senses on a self-led retreat. No matter where your retreat is going to take place, having a beautiful bunch or bunches of flowers in your sacred space will lift your spirit and heart, and can remind you of your intention every time you catch a glimpse of them.

Food and snacks – This is a vitally important part of your retreat planning, even if you plan on staying in a hotel and eating there the whole time. Eating is an opportunity to truly nourish yourself inside and out, so plan wholesome meals and drinks (you might even like to prepare some dishes ahead of time to take) and take time planning and procuring a shopping list of healthy, nutritious and decadent snacks to take with you. You might like to add lemon or mint to the water you drink, or select some nourishing herbal teas that complement your retreat intention (for example, a relaxing cup of chamomile tea). If you wish to partake in the "Simple tea ritual" in Chapter Three (see Rituals and practices), you will need either dried or fresh tea leaves. You might also wish to purchase some ceremonial grade, sustainably sourced cacao to practise the "Heart-opening ritual" or to enjoy as a hot cup of yum throughout your retreat. Make sure you also have ample fresh fruit available to you.

Images – You might like to gather some images ahead of your retreat, like photographs, printed images or magazine clippings. They can be displayed on an altar (see "Seasonal nature altar practice", Chapter Three – Mindfulness, nature and movement practices) or a mirror to help you stay connected to your retreat intention. You could include images of an ancestor whose energy you wish to connect with during the retreat, something you wish to manifest or a photo of yourself in a happy place.

Incense – There are a huge variety of incense fragrances, and it's often a case of trial and error to find one that suits you. Burning incense has been a widely-used practice in religious and spiritual ceremonies, and is synonymous with New Age practices today. The waft of some burning incense outside a yoga studio will instantly switch you into a different gear, and the act of lighting an incense stick can have the same effect. It can signify a threshold, which can come in handy during your retreat.

Journal – This is an essential tool for any retreat, but especially for a self-led retreat. I always suggest buying a new one for each retreat, using it to plan for, and during and after your retreat. It doesn't have to be fancy or expensive, but it helps if it is a pleasing colour or delights you in some way. I personally have a thing for pretty journals and when I've filled one up, I truly delight in shopping for the next one.

Oracle cards – Bringing a trusted deck of oracle cards or treating yourself to a new one can be a powerful tool for self-reflection and spiritual connection. You might like to pull a card at the start and end of your retreat as you practise your opening and closing ceremonies. You might also feel called to pull a card during journalling practices or to help you stay focused and connected, bringing you back to the intentional experience of being on retreat.

Palo santo (ethically sourced) – Burning a stick of palo santo is an alternative to burning sage, but is used in the same way. It carries a slightly sweeter smell, which is considered less intense than sage smoke. Having access to a stick of palo santo can aid meditation on your retreat and beyond. Just note that there are growing concerns over use of palo santo and deforestation, so ensure you look for ethically or sustainably sourced sticks. "Palo santo" translates as "holy wood", and the *Bursera graveolens* tree (known in Spanish as "palo santo") is native to South American countries, and is often used in shamanic rituals and practices. Traditionally, the spirit of the tree is released when it dies, and it is the burning of the dead wood that holds the power.

Pens or pencils – I love a stationery shop and love nothing more than coloured pens and highlighters. Whether it's a colourful array of pens or just a handful of decent ones, making sure you come armed with a few is key. There is nothing worse than arriving at your self-led retreat ready for some self-reflection and realising the one pen you bought with you has just run out.

Playlist – Create yourself a playlist ahead of your retreat with music that will help you relax, re-energise and stay focused. Or, you can listen to a playlist I've created for you called "The Retreat Yourself Book Playlist".

Sage stick – A sage stick is a bundle of dried sage leaves. The smoke released when the leaves are burned is used to energetically cleanse spaces and people due to its antibacterial and antimicrobial properties. You might like to buy a sage stick to have available for your retreat, although bear in mind if you are in a hotel, burning sage in your room will not be allowed. Burning sage as a means of spiritually cleansing yourself and connecting with the spirit of nature has been a practice among Indigenous tribes spanning the globe. From Indigenous American tribes to European witches, sage has been used in daily rituals and larger ceremonial practices for centuries.

Spell candles – These are small candles that burn relatively quickly. They often come in various colours, which are attuned to whatever it is you are interested in manifesting or feeling. There are many places online where you can find spell candles made by artisan makers and small businesses.

Toiletries and products – I love delicious-smelling products, and like to make sure I pack things I love that feel luxurious. While you don't need to break the bank and buy the most expensive products, it is nice to treat yourself to what you can. Whether it's a body oil, a face mask or bubble bath, reflect on what you might like to bring with you to aid your retreat experience. There is guidance for a ritual bath in the "Ritual bath" practice in Chapter Three (see Rituals and practices), and a good quality body oil or massage oil is also recommended, particularly if you choose to practice the "Body love ritual" also in that chapter.

Yoga mat – You don't need a yoga mat to practise yoga, but using one can not only offer comfort and support for your joints, but it can also create a sacred space to practise. If you don't have one, you can also use a towel, or any comfortable natural surface like soft spongy grass (just make sure you don't slip).

Checklist

Having worked through this chapter you should now have the following in place:

- ☐ A retreat intention
- ☐ A venue booked
- ☐ A date secured
- ☐ Your "retreat yourself" tool kit items planned
- ☐ Your retreat meals, drinks and snacks planned

THE RUMANIAN PLAIN

Chapter Three

Curating your retreat activities

You have a date and a venue booked. You have an idea of what it is you need right now. And you know what you would like to explore further during your retreat. Now, it's time to create a rough plan of what you would like to do during your retreat. If you were joining a group retreat, a schedule of activities would be carefully selected and scheduled for you. But on your self-led retreat, you get to choose what you practise matched specifically to your own individual needs.

Throughout this chapter, you will be offered a menu of options that includes rituals, readings, and movement, nature and self-reflection practices. You are invited to select a few of these practices based on what calls to you and what best suits your needs right now. The number of practices will depend on how long your retreat is, but the key to any retreat is to not cram a schedule full, but instead to leave plenty of space. It is in this open, unplanned, unhurried reflective space that often the insights, wisdom and moments of profound self-connection are able to surface or form.

Rituals and practices

Rituals and ceremonies have been an important part of community, family and personal life journeys across the globe for centuries but have become lost in the busyness of modern Western culture. Often, ceremonies and rituals are reserved for the big moments in life, such as a wedding ceremony, graduation or religious ceremonies of various kinds. The difference between a ritual and a ceremony is that a ritual is a set of conscious and intentional actions that are performed regularly (sometimes daily) and a ceremony is a stand-alone event or sacred practice to mark an occasion or a crossing of a threshold. Sacred moments, rites of passage and crossings of a threshold happen all the time in our daily lives, but often we are too busy, racing through life to not notice and honour those priceless moments.

Retreat opening ceremony

Holding a simple ceremony to mark the start of your retreat can be an intentional way to cross a threshold into a different energy and mindset. It's a moment where you can consciously draw a line between the outside world and your sacred retreat space in order to embody the essence and energy of being on a retreat, which is about being present, open, focused and intentional.

Practise this ritual once you've arrived in your chosen space, unpacked, set up your space, had a drink and feel ready to begin. Follow the simple steps opposite and adapt to suit your own desires and needs.

You will need:

a sage stick, palo santo or an aura or room cleansing spray; a lighter or matches (optional); a candle; your journal and a pen; and any other tools from your tool kit that you'd like (like flowers, crystals or incense).

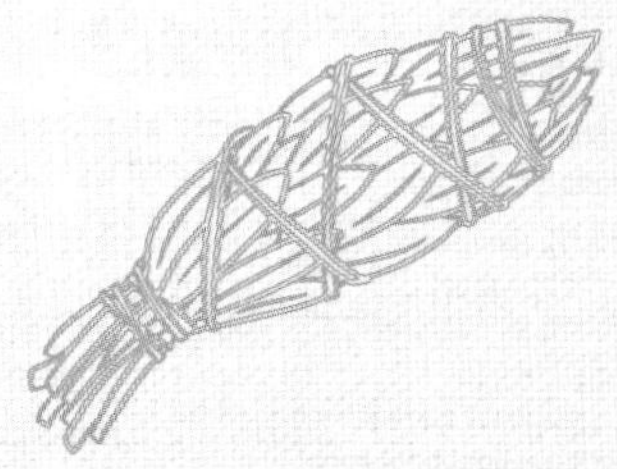

The ritual

- Cleanse the space you are in with a sage stick or palo santo stick (if permitted) or an aura or room cleansing spray.
- Open your journal and write down your intention.
- Grab any other tools from your tool kit that you wish to bring into the space. Arrange all items intentionally on the floor or table.
- Take a seat on the floor or at a table and take a deep breath.
- When you are ready to begin your opening ceremony, light a candle to symbolise the start.
- Place both hands over your heart, close your eyes and become aware of your heart space.
- Spend a few minutes in meditation focusing on your heart space and your breath. Soften your shoulders and jaw and notice if you can feel your energy grounding in your body and into the space you are in.
- When you are ready, say out loud "I give myself permission to [state your intention]. I am here now, right where I am meant to be. I promise myself I will remain present throughout this experience and I know I am worthy of it. I invite protective, loving energy and guides into this space with me. Thank you for this time and space, I am ready to fully be here now".
- Say any additional affirmations that feel right and relevant to you and your experience.
- Take a long, slow deep breath and open the palms of your hands so that they face upward in a receptive gesture. Smile and open your eyes.
- To signify the end of your ceremony and the start of your retreat, safely blow the candle out.

Heart-opening cacao ritual

Intentionally working with cacao is a beautiful practice. Cacao is a potent form of plant medicine that is drunk ceremonially to energetically open and heal the heart and boost mood by activating the heart chakra. Some research suggests that drinking cacao can act as an antioxidant, have anti-inflammatory effects on the cardiovascular system and have physiological as well as energetic benefits for the heart.

Your heart-opening cacao ritual starts as soon as you begin to prepare the cacao drink. This is because stirring your intentions into the mixture as you prepare the drink is a vital part of the ritual, making it a mindfulness practice from start to finish.

You will need:

a solid block of ceremonial grade, single origin, ethically sourced drinking cacao; a chopping board; a sharp knife; a mug's worth of milk, milk alternative or water; a saucepan; a sweetener of your choice, like honey or maple syrup; a whisk; your favourite mug; a candle; and a lighter or matches.

The ritual

- Centre yourself by taking few deep breaths, and feeling your feet planted firmly on the ground.
- Bring your intention to mind (or choose a new one for this ritual) and, on a chopping board, start to slice thin flakes of cacao from the block. Two tablespoons of cacao flakes should be enough, but you can adjust the quantity to suit your own taste.
- Place the milk, milk alternative or water into the saucepan and bring to a simmer.
- Add the flakes of raw cacao.
- Whisk the cacao and imagine pouring blessings, gratitude and your intention into the cacao mix, stirring the energy in as you go. Stir until the cacao has fully dissolved into a smooth silky texture.
- Add a splash of sweetener to suit your taste and mix in.
- When the mixture is fully blended, pour the cacao drink into your mug and take a seat on the floor.
- Light a candle before cradling the warm mug with both hands in front of your heart.
- Close your eyes and engage your heart space by holding your focus there. Conjure up feelings of love and gratitude from within, and slowly sip your cacao, imagining the drink healing and soothing your heart. Do this slowly and mindfully for as long as it takes for you to finish the drink.
- Once finished, place the cup down, take a deep breath and imagine your heart opening and pulsing with love and light.
- When you are ready, open your eyes and blow the candle out safely.

Manifesting your desires ritual

Manifesting is not about materialism. It's about conjuring up and embodying a feeling and an energy that will attract the same energy back to you, according to the laws of the universe. It's an ever-evolving practice of inner and outer work, and a journey toward self-knowledge, intentional decision making and aligning our lives with our deepest values.

The first thing you'll need to do for this ritual is to get as clear and specific as possible about what it is you want to manifest (what you want to experience in your life). You might like to ask yourself: how would I like to feel? This is manifesting: embodying a feeling to be a co-pilot with the universe to bring your physical reality up to match it. Manifesting is about presence as much as it is about allowing yourself to dream and want what you want.

You will need:

calming music (optional); a sage stick, palo santo stick or an aura or room cleansing spray; a lighter or matches; a spell candle or tea light; and images of what you'd like to manifest (optional).

The ritual

- Bring to mind the thing you would like to manifest. You might like to play some calming music from your playlist during this practice.
- Cleanse yourself by carefully wafting a sage stick or palo santo stick around your body, or spraying an aura or room cleansing spray around you.
- Dim the lights and place the spell candle or tea light in front of you on a table. If you have brought images of what you'd like to manifest with you, place these on the table too.
- When you are ready, sit down and light the candle to signify the start of your manifesting practice.
- Close your eyes and take three deep breaths.
- Bring to mind what you would like to manifest, and imagine yourself embodying or experiencing it. See yourself as happy, fulfilled, grateful and full of love. Allow this image or scene to conjure up the exact feelings in the here and now as if it is real. Marinate in these feelings, allowing them to grow stronger and more vivid as the practice goes on.
- When you feel ready to bring the practice to a close, say "Thank you" out loud three times, as if thanking the universe for already having delivered your manifestation to you.
- Allow the candle to burn out on its own accord. Do not blow it out! Once the candle is extinguished, the spell or manifesting ritual has been cast.

Morning ritual

A morning ritual is the best way to intentionally start your day. It is such a nourishing and empowering way to anchor into the presence, to engage the heart and to help you move through your day with a greater sense of awareness, grace and peace. You might like to practise this every morning during your self-led retreat, and this might be something you take forward into your daily life (see more on this in Chapter Five: Integration).

You can play around with ideas for this practice to suit your own needs and desires, which can develop over time. But here is a suggested ritual to get you started. Don't worry about getting it right. Simply choose something that engages mind, body and soul in a nourishing, intentional way.

This ritual is a great opportunity to re-engage with your retreat intention. What would best serve you right now to set your day up in the most delicious way?

You will need:

a glass of water (placed beside your bed the night before the ritual); a book of your choice; a candle; a lighter or matches; a timer; and your journal and a pen.

The ritual

- As soon as you stir in the morning, say "Thank you for this day" out loud.
- Take some time to luxuriate in the comfort of the bed before swinging your legs over the side of the bed. Pause here with your feet on the ground, take three deep breaths. Then, take a few sips of the glass of water.
- Slowly rise to a standing position before spending a few moments feeling into the sensations of the body.
- Comb your fingers across your scalp, and rub your face and jaw.
- Rub your shoulders and down your arms, and shake your hands out.
- Rub your body along the front, back and sides of your chest, tummy and back.
- Finally, rub your hands down each leg to your feet, shaking each leg out in turn.
- Take a big overhead stretch and shake your whole body.
- Pick up your book of choice, come to a seated position on the floor and read a short poem or passage. Read mindfully and allow the words to fill you up.
- Next, on a steady surface, set a timer for 10 minutes and light a candle. Lighting the candle will signify the start of a short breath meditation.
- Close your eyes and take your awareness to your breath. Notice the sensations of each breath as it comes and goes. Hold your awareness on the breath as an anchor for the duration of the meditation. If your mind wanders, simply drop the thought and return to your breath.
- When the timer sounds, pick up your journal and spend another 10 minutes journalling your thoughts in an unedited stream of consciousness (often referred to as automatic writing).
- Come back up to a standing position and take one more stretch, before repeating out loud "Thank you for this day".

Validating emotions rituals

Rejecting or denying yours or others' negative emotions is referred to as emotional or spiritual bypassing. But there is a misconception that, in order to be spiritual or a "good" person, we must only feel "love and light", which is harmful narrative that can lead to shame and guilt when we experience emotions such as anger, envy, bitterness or frustration.

One of the most powerful moments of change in my life was when I realised that I rarely, if ever, validated my own feelings. When I realised I had a dysfunctional relationship with validating my emotions, I realised it wasn't just negative emotions I struggled to validate, but "good" or positive ones too, such as hope or love.

When we deny or ignore our emotions, they will always find another way to express themselves in subtle, unconscious and often more harmful ways. This can lead to harmful habits or addictions; physically through illness or disease; or through sleep problems, anxiety and depression. It can also lead you to feel disconnected from your "self", leading to feelings of stagnation, dissolution or social exclusion.

If this is something you struggle with, you can use the time and space of your retreat to explore your own relationship with this, and start to cultivate the skill of internal emotional validation. To validate your own emotions, you have to acknowledge, accept and be with both the "good" and "bad" emotions, without judgement. This requires you to witness your emotions and to get curious about them.

Meditation and journalling are excellent self-led tools for developing this skill, as is therapy (if this is an option available to you). But here are two practices you can get started with during your retreat:

Mindfulness ritual

When experiencing an emotion with mindfulness, you can more easily create space between you and the feeling, which can help you to view the emotion as something you are experiencing, rather than something you are.

- Take a deep breath and notice what emotion is present for you.
- Name the emotion and say to yourself "Right now, I am experiencing [insert emotion]".
- Notice if the emotion carries a physical sensation in your body. For example, in your heart, stomach or facial muscles. Some people may resonate with visualising the emotion they are experiencing as a colour.
- Place your hand on your heart and say to yourself "It's ok to feel [insert emotion]" or "It's safe to feel [insert emotion]". Whichever resonates with you most.
- Finish by expressing the energy of the emotion in some way. For example, you could shake your hands out, take a nap, self-hug your body, laugh or scream into a pillow.

Journalling ritual

Journalling is a way of witnessing and expressing your emotions in a safe and contained way. Through a journalling practice, you can dig a little deeper into why you might be feeling a certain way, what was the trigger, what part of you feels intimidated, scared or intrigued by that emotion.

Explore, through journalling, all angles of the emotion and your relationship to it. Through doing this, watch the emotion loosen its grip it has on you in the present moment. All you need is your journal and a pen.

- Pick up your journal and pen and write out, as a stream of consciousness, what emotions are present for you in the moment. Get curious, and stay loving.

Ritual bath

Taking a ritual bath or shower can feel like a luxurious act of self-care, and is a perfect ritual for a self-led retreat. While most of us bathe every day, we tend to do so habitually out of a necessity to be clean. This is, of course, an act of self-care in itself, but not necessarily a conscious one. At the start of this book, we explored how an intention has the power to turn the mundane into something sacred. A ritual bath is a perfect example of this.

There are a vast range of ingredients you can bring into your ritual bathing experience, but the most powerful and potent ones aren't physical; it is the intention, level of presence and gratitude you bring into the experience.

The key to a bathing ritual is to engage your senses with a focus on nourishment, and feeding your body, mind and soul.

You will need:

candles; a lighter or matches; bathing tools of your choice (like bath salts, essential oils, herbs or flowers); your preferred body cleansing items; a soothing soundtrack; a sage stick or an aura or room cleansing spray (optional); a bath towel; and body oil or lotion.

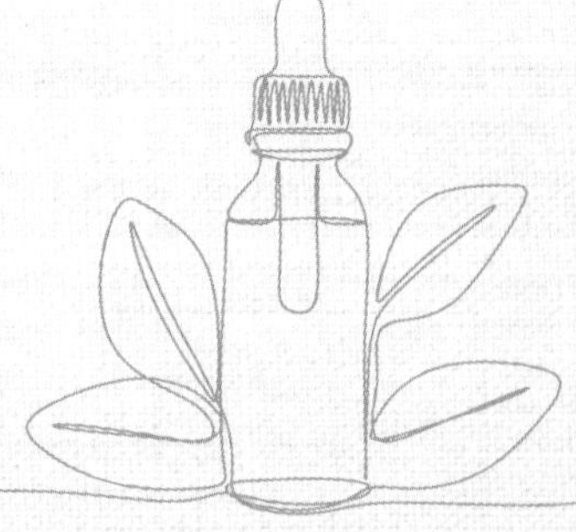

The ritual

- Click play on your soothing soundtrack.
- If you choose to, cleanse the space you are in with a sage stick or an aura or room cleansing spray.
- To get set up, dim the lights, light your candles, and gather any bathing tools from your tool kit.
- Begin to run your bath, and as you are pouring in any ingredients, bring an intention to mind and imagine it infusing the water.
- Once your bath is ready, take your time getting into the bath. Move slowly and mindfully and become aware of the sensation of the water touching your skin, and the sensation of your body immersing in it.
- Once you are submerged, feel a sense of gratitude for the sacred gift of water and say "Thank you".
- Slowly and mindfully wash your whole body. Do so with tenderness and gratitude, lingering over any parts of your body that are tense or tight, like the shoulders. You might like to have your eyes closed as you do this.
- Allow your body to soak in the warmth of the water and imagine every cell being cleansed.
- Allow your awareness to rest on the music playing or the flicker of the candle, and stay soaking and resting for at least 15 minutes.
- When you are ready to get out, do so carefully, slowly and mindfully.
- Dry yourself and take your time to moisturise your whole body with a delicious smelling body oil or lotion.

Simple tea ritual

A tea ritual can be a beautiful way of connecting to the power of plants and nature. Tea rituals are found in many cultures around the world, and all seem to have one thing in common: a sense of bringing together and connecting.

Tea rituals are so common we might not even realise we are taking part in them. For example, making tea in the morning in the same way in the same cup is a ritual, as is flicking the kettle on to brew some tea as soon as a friend or guest enters your home. There is something about tea that feels ceremonial and comforting, and on your self-led retreat, a tea ritual can help you reconnect with nature and the wild part of yourself.

For this ritual, your tea leaves can be foraged or shop-bought, but if you have access to fresh mint or nettles, I would recommend using these for your ritual. Nettle leaves can be harvested from around February to October in the Northern Hemisphere, and foraging for them can be an enjoyable activity to add to your retreat schedule. Mint is a perennial that tends to grow all year round. Cleavers or "sticky weed" is another easily accessible hedgerow plant you can forage and brew to make a healing tea.

You will need:

a mug; a kettle of hot water; fresh or dried tea leaves of your choice; tea strainer (optional); a candle; a lighter or matches; and music or nature sounds (optional).

Caution: When foraging, always wear gloves (especially when foraging nettles); wash materials thoroughly before consuming them; never pick anything you can't 100 per cent identify; and pick ethically and responsibly, with permission from any landowners, and mindfulness of your surroundings. If you are unsure whether any of these herbs are suitable for you; you are pregnant or taking medication; or have sensitive skin or allergies, please consult a doctor before ingesting any of the ingredients suggested here.

The ritual

- Select a pleasing mug and boil the kettle.
- Add your tea to the mug. If you are using fresh leaves, add a handful of washed leaves (adjusting the amount of leaves to your own taste). If you are using shop-bought leaves you may wish to use a strainer. Once the kettle has boiled, pour the hot water over the leaves.
- Take your time to brew your chosen leaves slowly, and watch the leaves move and dance in the water. Reflect on the journey of the leaves from their origin to this moment.
- While the tea is still brewing, light a candle. You might also wish to play background music or nature sounds.
- Once your tea has brewed, raise the mug to your nose, and take a breath in to notice any fragrance. Notice what that fragrance does to your body and mind. Repeat this three times, taking three deep, mindful breaths.
- When the tea is cool enough to drink, take a sip and notice the flavours, sipping slowly and mindfully.
- If you can, see if you can notice what beneficial qualities the leaves have on your body, mind or soul. This will get easier with practise, but see if you can attune to the healing power of the leaves, and of nature. What is nature giving you through the leaves? Communing with the leaves in this way can help reconnect you to the wild nature found within, helping to remind you we are part of, not separate from, nature.
- When you have finished your tea, spend a few moments looking at the tea leaves at the bottom of the cup. Is there a message you can decipher from there too?

Body love ritual

When the skin and muscles of our bodies are massaged, endorphins are released, offering a boost in mood and a reduction in stress hormones. A massage received by a trained therapist is one of my favourite self-care treats. But the nerve cells of the body cannot tell the difference between a massage coming from someone else or from ourselves, meaning a self-massage is an equally powerful self-care option.

If a paid-for massage is not something available to you as part of your self-led retreat, but you would still like to feel the benefits of a massage, this simple body loving ritual is a great alternative option that will leave you feeling relaxed, held and good. This can be a beautiful practice to combine with a ritual bath or the ritual foot soak (see Chapter Three – Rituals and practices).

You will need:

loose-fitting clothing; a sage stick or an aura or room cleansing spray; a lighter or matches; cushions, bolsters or blankets; incense or candles; spa music; and a massage oil or carrier oil (like coconut oil or virgin olive oil).

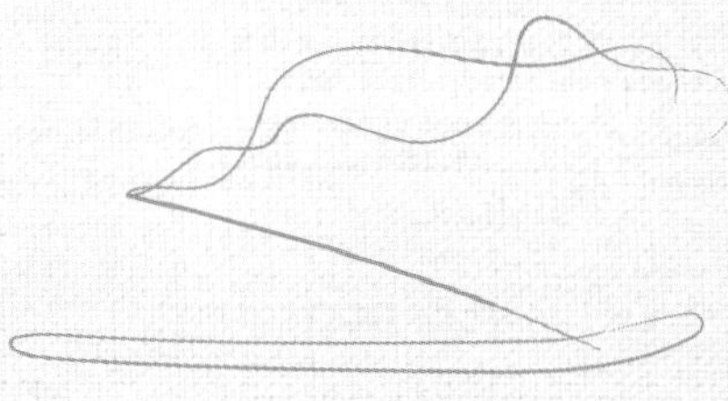

The ritual

- Wearing loose-fitting clothing, begin by cleansing yourself and the space you are in with a sage stick or an aura or room cleansing spray.
- Set up a comfortable space on the floor using cushions, bolsters and blankets. Light some incense or candles, and play some spa music.
- Come down to a seated position on the floor in the comfy nest you've made, making sure your massage oil is close to hand.
- Allow your breath to find a natural, easy rhythm. Practise a few minutes of a body scan meditation, taking your awareness from your head down to your toes. Consciously relax any tension you find while doing this.
- Close your eyes, take your fingertips to your hairline and start to gently massage your scalp. Notice what pressure and movement feels good to you, and focus on how it feels to receive and stay connected to your breath. Continue massaging for as long as it feels good to.
- Massage your forehead, massage the temples and jaw.
- Adding a few drops of your oil to your fingertips, start to massage the back of your neck, noticing what pressure feels good and nourishing. Don't rush.
- Adding a little more oil to your hands if needed, reach for your left shoulder, allowing your left arm to become completely relaxed. Massage your right shoulder, then slowly massage down the right arm and hand.
- Repeat on the left side, adding more oil if needed.
- Continue to massage down your body, focusing on the top of your chest, the parts of your back you are able to reach, and each leg and foot in turn. Add more oil when needed, and move slowly and mindfully.
- When you have finished, sit in meditation for around five minutes. Notice how your body and heart feels.
- Close the ritual with a long slow in breath, and an audible sigh out.

Ritual foot soak

We often forget to acknowledge how hard our feet work, and that they quite literally carry us through our days. Not only are our feet taken for granted, but prioritising them in a self-care practice is often overlooked. Soaking and massaging the feet not only feels great, but it can also stimulate powerful acupressure points, having a balancing and positive effect on the whole body.

You might have had a reflexology treatment before, where a trained professional works with the acupressure points on your feet with the intention of bringing the body, mind and soul into balance. Massaging your own feet can stimulate and work with these same points. If there is something specific you'd like to work on, you can easily look up which specific acupressure points to massage or apply pressure to. Otherwise, just intuitively work on your feet, lingering where it feels particularly good or important.

You will need:

a washing-up bowl full of warm water (or a bath filled up to ankle height with warm water); a chair; your choice of bath salts, essential oils, herbs or flowers; a hand towel; massage oil or lotion; and a book or passage of text of your choosing (this can include one of the readings from Chapter Three – Readings).

The ritual

- Set up a comfy seat and place the bowl of warm water at the foot of the chair. Or, if you are using a bath for this ritual, come to the side of the bath.
- Pour your chosen salts, essential oils, herbs or flowers into the water and bless the water by saying "May these minerals and herbs purify and nourish me. Thank you for nature's gifts. I am ready to receive". Adapt or add to the words of this blessing as you see fit.
- Come to sit on the chair or side of the bath.
- Dip the toes on one foot into the water and slowly immerse the whole foot. Then, repeat this, slowly adding the second foot into the water until both are submerged.
- Close your eyes and take a few rounds of deep breaths.
- Spend a few minutes with your eyes closed and your feet soaking, focusing on the subtle sensation of water on your feet and the connection of your feet to the earth. Notice a sense of grounding and cleansing as you rest here for a while.
- Next, pick up your sacred text and read a passage, reading or poem out loud.
- Close your eyes again and reflect on the sentiment of the words you have spoken, allowing them to vibrate through your body and soul.
- When you are ready, take your feet out of the water, towel dry each foot and take your time to mindfully massage each foot in turn using your massage oil or lotion. Put gentle pressure on the soles of your feet, your toes, heels, the tops of your feet and your ankles. Focus on areas that feel good and pour a sense of gratitude into your feet as you go.

Skin-care ritual

A facial can not only be deeply relaxing, but it also stimulates blood flow, ridding the skin of toxins. You might apply moisturiser to your face once or twice a day, but if you're like most people, it is done so in a hurry without much thought. Making skin-care a ritual can act as a powerful mindfulness practice, especially as washing or moisturising our faces usually happens as one of the first and/or last things we do each day.

Turning the mundane into a sacred practice in this ritual can help anchor your day in intention, purpose and love, so consider practising this short skin-care ritual each morning and evening of your retreat.

You will need:

a mirror; a facial wash or cleanser; a flannel or face cloth; a face towel; and a facial moisturiser.

If you packed a face mask in your "retreat yourself" tool kit, you might also like to bring that into this ritual.

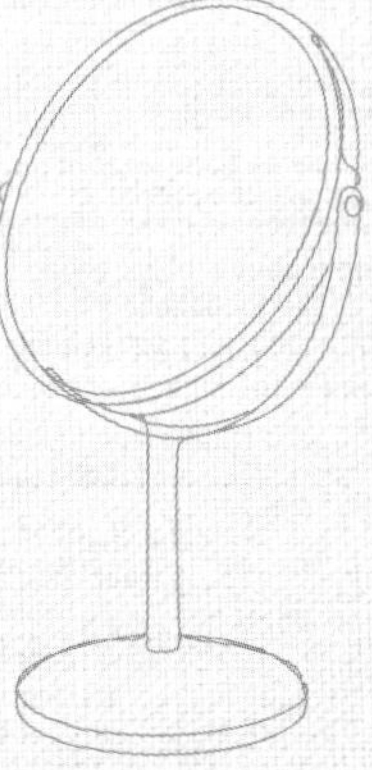

The ritual

- Stand with your feet planted firmly on the ground at the bathroom sink, facing a mirror.
- Close your eyes and notice how your body feels. Do you feel balanced, wobbly, rested or tired?
- Take a deep breath, then sigh the breath back out making an audible sound.
- Open your eyes and look in the mirror. Gently smile, and say, eye-to-eye with yourself in the mirror, "I love you, I'm proud of you, I am here".
- Place a little bit of facial wash or cleanser in the palms of your hands and rub them together. Bring your hands up to your nose and take a few long, slow inhales, noticing any scent or fragrance.
- Slowly and mindfully massage your face with the cleanser. Do so tenderly and not in a hurry. It might feel good to gently massage the jaw or the muscles around your eyes, including the space between the eyebrows.
- Wet the flannel or face cloth with warm water and place it gently over your face. Move with tenderness again as you remove the facial wash or cleanser, before gently patting your face dry with a towel.
- Apply your facial moisturiser with the same sense of unhurried tenderness, closing your eyes as you slowly allow the mixture to be absorbed, and gently massaging any areas that feel good to do so.
- Place your hands over your heart, take a few more deep breaths and bring your intention for the retreat (or the day) to mind.
- Close your ritual by opening your eyes and repeating the affirmation "I love you, I'm proud of you, I'm here".

Readings

Reading poetry is a meditation. A poem, verse or reading written from the heart and from a place of truth has the power to conjure up feelings and emotions in a unique way. Poetry can act as a mirror or a signpost, offer comfort or help people feel seen and understood. Using poetry, prose or readings as a mindfulness, spiritual or self-connection practice throughout your self-led retreat can help keep you anchored to your intention, to the present moment and to your own feeling of self-connection. You might even find that reading poetry or prose unlocks doors within you to begin writing yourself.

In this section, you will find a collection of poetry and prose to support you during your retreat. You might like to start or close your day reading one that you have carefully selected, or you might like to open a page at random points throughout your retreat for guidance, comfort or support.

From my heart to yours. I hope these words bring you a sense of comfort and peace

The deepest acceptance

I got lost for a moment, excavating the past to find answers
getting caught in a web of thoughts of what was lacking or what could have been
I got lost in thought of a future that has not yet arrived
of what I have not yet achieved or become
forgetting all I'd uncovered in awareness
the peace of present moment
waiting patiently – always – for me to return

anchored in presence
I know there is nothing to heal, change or become
the freedom of knowing – I am and all is
it's in presence i feel the deepest acceptance
anchored in here i feel my foundation
my eyes lift to the horizon as the corners of my mouth turn up
my heart expands in my chest

the past was perfect – it led me here
and the future is flooded with light

Divine feminine rising

going slower than usual

gathering scattered parts of me back

landing fully in body, planting feet in the earth remembering – be, don't do

soothing the part of me so used to the chase

untangling the tentacles of energy entrapped in the masculine world of
accumulating, building, doing doing doing

bringing it all back – to heart, womb, eyes, lips, fingertips

pulled by feminine energy to rest

to find my centre deeper than ever before and start again

body, soul, heart exhausted by old ways

it is time ~ she is rising ~

with the real work yet to come

we are all being called

surrendering to it I gather, ground and remake a promise

to anchor every thought in intention, feed every cell with love

wait for the call to action in ways I don't even know yet

the divine feminine is rising

To be love

I forgot

to look to the night sky to remember

to notice the dew on each blade of grass as i plant my feet on the earth,
just to breathe

I forgot

to expand my awareness to the vastness of all creation

to remember my place in the cycle of all things

short, precious, a miracle

I forgot

not to believe the narrow judgements the mind's perception

to not be consumed by the to-dos and wanting to please

and the feeling of being not quite good enough

I forgot

the undercurrent of what exists without my trying

which bring true beauty, peace and healing to light

I forgot i am made of the same stuff as stars

the dew, the earth, the breeze at dawn

I forgot, for a moment

to be love

Thank you for this day

• feel •

breathe into your heart

make it a living enquiry

ask: how am I today?

• soften •

breathe into the whole body

expand every cell with life

notice: what is my body trying to say?

• be •

breathe into dark corners

flood every part of you with light

you are worthy as you are of your own love

• live •

imagine your eyes smiling

your heart smiling – every cell in the body smiling

turn the corners of your mouth up

and whisper

thank you for this day

The search

I was searching for home in all the wrong places
in a person, a place or a role
mistaking that, once found, I could grasp them to make them mine
effort to hold what is impermanent, as permanent
believing then, there is something to lose
I realise now
home is right here
in the ocean of light within my chest
always there
and accessible
nothing then to seek but instead to notice
what I'm already a part of
finding peace in remembering
there is nothing to lose

Trusting life

dreams are as fluid
as the f l o w of a river
an unconscious draw of journey
calling us into life

each bend, twist and turn
each arrival at a dreamed up destination
simply reveals more of the journey ahead

yet the river doesn't settle
or mistake a lake for the ocean
the river never knew of the vastness that awaits

and so I will keep on dreaming
with hands over my heart in gratitude
for all that's been
all that is yet to come

trusting the flow of a river that carries me
to living this life into life

Home

I've come to know my own heart
and accept all I can see
and to love what's still in hiding
the shadow side of me

i've come to know my longings
my hopes, my fears, my dreams
to trust and sense my own truth
when all's not what it seems

i've come to know potential
the limitless and free
I've come to feel what love is
a greater force than me

i've come to a surrender
the "I am" truth behind it all
no separation but a oneness
of the caller and the call

Finding balance

returning to stillness she finds her centre

to live this life – the middle way

seeking the space where the pendulum balances effortlessly between light and shade

joy and sadness

she learned not to grasp hold of elation

when life is going her way

but instead to savour it

nor believe in times of challenge, that that too is fixed

instead she remembers

"this too shall pass"

to accept and find beauty in impermanence

as a reminder in each moment to live

in stillness she becomes curious

her heart opens with trust

like a flower in the warmth of light in spring

it's in stillness she takes a thousand steps

The horizon

the horizon is the beginning
where known meets unknown
two worlds collide
forever reaching into mystery
down into an underworld
and out to infinite energy just pretending to be
past and future bound together in the holding, the balance of equanimity
a mirror to this moment, right now – all that seems real
yet nothing is really known
just potential meeting story
mystery meeting mineral
a calling
to trust
to look forward
to keep moving forward
freedom is a surrender
it is to remember
to relinquish control of thinking I know how life should be
it's an arrival into trust
the deepest acceptance
that "now" is the opportunity
eyes up
heart open
trusting all is as it's meant to be

When the dark night comes

when the dark night comes, become like winter
strip yourself bare in truth and vulnerability
settle your animal body to the earth and lie still, breathing
let the snow land and melt like kisses on your tired limbs
the wind hush you to surrender
it's ok – let go – you'll remember
trust yourself to the darkness when it arrives
on the darkest night the sky can fill with the brightest stars
light signatures of time
dancing, as they do
to remind us of our place and space in this mystical unfolding
reminding us to look up – make a wish – remember the divine
the darkest night gives way the brightest dawn
and there is no rush
new life waits patiently beneath the frost
so much beauty found in a slow and gentle thaw
the light of a thousand rainbows held in each melted drop as it falls
so if the dark night arrives – you can smile
because deep down you'll remember the darkness just means a new dawn is coming
the darkness is not to be feared or resisted but instead to be realised
nature's perfect opportunity
to rest, transform, to be reborn
the dark night is our soul's surrender

Be here now

not a moment of this am I taking for granted

not a moment will I miss through misplaced thought

of what I've not yet become

it's here in each breath that I vow to live

d i s s o l v e d in the simplicity of each fluid moment

it's here in the vast expanse of presence

I find the freedom I'd been searching for

I promise now

I promise

I will not miss a thing

Still standing

everything has changed, yet here you are, getting through it
stronger, kinder, wiser from the storm
routines changed, structures crumbled
normality dissipated
yet here you are
still standing
finding your way in a temporary new norm
take a moment to breathe
notice the fertile earth beneath your feet
no need to fear this moment
but instead, choose wisely where you place your next step, and who for
remember your solid foundation – awareness
for this is love
always there, always waiting for you to return
do not waste a moment fearing what might come next but remember
you are here
still standing
breathe down into your roots
make that one wise, loving choice
in the direction of love, not fear
given the gift of time and space
a privilege
to love those we care for and care for those we love
to form new and meaningful routines

this experience, just as any, is temporary
the ever changing reality of life
yet here you are
still standing
finding home in the beating heart in your chest
safety in your feet planted on the earth
connection on levels perhaps you had forgotten
hope carried in the current of intention
relax into your tree-like foundation
breathe into your heart as a beacon of light and love
eyes to the horizon and focus on that one foot
placed compassionately, intentionally, generously in front of the other
remember your place
this web of divine connection
our collective pain, joy and strength
washed clean in awareness
space to notice
time to remember
all that you're a part of
all you've come through
because, look, here you are
still standing

As I am

and then, I surrendered
freed myself from the burden of trying
to become more than I am
let go of striving
to be just that little bit more
I sunk my roots deep
felt into the abundance that already surrounds me
and gasped for air
as if waking in a dream
breathing
for the first time in a while
I arrived home
in this body
exactly as I am

It's going to be ok

it's ok

breathe

for a moment lay down your weapons

remove the armour that you've held on so tightly

unspoken words, unkept promises, actions taken in fear

all resisting the very peace that you seek

surrendered now at your feet

it's ok

breathe right into the centre of your chest

breathe it into opening

unshackle your feet from the chains of what could have been

or what scares you about the unfolding of a new way

held in this space, this time, this moment of surrender

it's ok

unbound, bare and held by pure light

heart expanding with each new breath

every arrival here a new version of you emerges

wiser, kinder, more loving

more at ease within your own skin

And as you meet yourself here

surrender a little more

don't be afraid

beautiful soul

it's ok

The middle way

awareness is an invitation to live an authentic life

to know that your life, your reality, is not fixed but instead is a vast expanse of endless possibilities

it's an invitation to believe in your dreams, your abilities and to know you are worthy

to trust in all the adventures yet to be had, including the ones you have not yet imagined

awareness is an invitation to see clearly

to find home inside yourself

to find balance when the oceans are rough and to trust when the clouds descend

to feel aligned, strong, stable and at peace within yourself, for yourself and ultimately for others

awareness is your invitation to know that this moment, right now, is all that's real

this moment is the beginning

this moment leans forward and says "trust me"

awareness is your truth – your story – your new beginning

it reminds you to take responsibility, that it is only you who can step forward for yourself

but before you do, know we are all doing the same, we are right here with you

with our eyes open, our minds free and our hearts ready to receive
awareness is our invitation to move forward together

to be love

Mindfulness, nature and movement practices

The following simple practices will offer you the opportunity to get out into nature, move your body and deepen your connection to the present moment. Practising any of these practices during your retreat can help be a catalyst for embedding them into your daily life through the integration stage in Chapter Five. These are nourishing practices that should leave you feeling balanced, energised, calm and present. What a delicious state to be in during a retreat or in daily life.

Mindful day practice

When we make the mundane sacred with intention, our experience of life itself is transformed. Yet in the hustle and bustle of daily life, our ability to slip into automatic pilot mode and live out each day without paying much attention to it becomes our norm. Simple routines and habits are performed unconsciously, leading us to feel as if we're just going through the motions rather than truly living or experiencing life. The space and pace of a self-led retreat affords you the opportunity to practise a more conscious way of moving through your day. The way you perform your daily tasks – from your daily basic hygiene routines to preparing food, eating, exercising or resting – can be an opportunity for mindfulness, presence and self-care. This practice can be weaved through your self-led retreat from the start to finish, and it can act as a starting block to integrate this way of being into your daily life (more on this in Chapter Five: Integration).

The practice

- Choose an activity you will be doing as a given during your retreat (for example, eating).
- Set an intention to perform this activity mindfully for the duration of your retreat.
- Pause before you begin the activity and engage your five senses. With eating as an example, pause with the bowl of food or snack in front of you before you take a bite. Bring the bowl up to your nose and inhale the aromas. Notice the textures and colours of the food. Notice how you feel in your body. Are you relaxed? Are you present, or are you in a hurry? Notice whether your breathing is steady and even, or short and sharp. Take a small bite of the food and really notice the changing flavours. Take your time to chew.
- Really be with the experience of the activity you have chosen. You are not going to experience anything particularly wild or life changing in this one attempt, but what you are doing is setting a strong foundation for being able to stay present in an experience. With eating in mind, if you decide to do this with every meal during your retreat, you will notice that it is somewhat easier to stay present and awake throughout other activities, too.

Wisdom of trees practice

Spending time among the trees has significant benefits for mental and physical health. Forest bathing – a practice that originated in Japan as an antidote to the rising stress level among everyday people – is becoming more and more popular in the Western world. Simply taking yourself to and immersing yourself in a forest during your self-led retreat will offer you a multitude of benefits. There's nothing you need to do; you just need to take yourself there and let nature do the healing work for you! To deepen your practice, deepen your connection with nature and regulate your energy, you might also like to include the following practice as part of your retreat schedule.

The practice

- If you're able to be in a forest for this practice, great. If not, find a tree that you feel drawn to and have permissible access to. If you are in a forest, take a slow and mindful walk until you find a tree that you feel drawn to.
- Pause for a moment at the tree and notice the intricate detail of it. Get a sense of the age and wisdom of the tree. Reflect for a moment on all that it might have witnessed and the resilience it has weathered.
- Place one hand on the trunk of the tree and close your eyes. Focus on your steady, even breath. Spend a few moments here just being with the tree.
- Then, place your other hand over your heart. See if you can feel an energetic connection between your heart energy and the energy of the tree, while staying connected to your breath. The energy of established trees can often feel maternal or paternal, or like being with a safe, wise elder. Soak it up.
- Notice if any questions arise within you. Perhaps you are looking for a piece of advice; there is something you seek guidance on or encouragement with; or there is something you know you need to hear. Ask the tree for guidance and support with one hand on the trunk and one hand on your heart. Perhaps some intuitive inner wisdom arises from within.
- When it feels right, place both hands around the tree trunk in an embrace. Keep your eyes closed and breathe. Spend at least five minutes here – or however long feels comfortable to you – feeling held by the energy of the tree.
- When you are ready, take a deep breath, open your eyes and whisper "Thank you" to the tree.
- Step away and take a few moments to reorient yourself with the space that surrounds you. Take in the light, the movement and the magic of it all.
- You might like to reflect on the experience in your journal later.

Silent walking meditation practice

Getting out for a good stomp during your retreat is an excellent idea, no matter where you are. You will – by the very nature of being on self-led solo retreat – do this in silence. There are two modes you can walk in: the first is being fully present to the experience, alert to your surroundings and taking it all in; and the second is walking along consumed by thought, eyes down, not being present or noticing anything at all, instead, being in your head. During your retreat you'll be aspiring for the first mode.

If you take any kind of walk during your retreat, see it as an opportunity for a mindfulness meditation practice and to engage your senses and be fully present in your surroundings. This turns a simple walk into a mindfulness practice.

To deepen a walking practice further and use walking as a formal meditation practice, you might like to try the practice described here. This meditation practice is much like when you sit on a meditation cushion with your eyes closed, but it brings gentle, grounded movement into the experience.

The practice

- For this practice you don't need to go very far (in fact, this practice is traditionally practised walking in a small circle). Ideally you will have access to a small patch of earth or grass – a garden is perfect for this – or it can be on the beach, in the park or woods.
- If it's safe to do so, take your socks and shoes off so your feet are connected to the earth.
- Start the meditation standing still with both feet planted on the ground. Take your gaze down to the earth and half close your eyes. Notice how balanced you feel standing tall. Notice the connection of your feet to the earth. Become aware of the rhythm of your breath for a few moments. See if you can anchor into the present moment and allow a clear, spacious mind.
- Start to take one small step (but do so very slowly). Connect your heel to the earth first and slowly roll the rest of your foot to reconnect with the ground, staying connected to your breath and a spacious mind. Notice the sensation in your feet and throughout your whole body.
- Keep doing this slowly, step by step.
- When you notice your mind has wandered or is consumed by thought of anything other than your walking meditation, pause. Take a deep breath and reconnect to the sensations in your feet and body. Once you have regained a level of presence, continue with your walking meditation. This is the practice: a slow-moving walking meditation.
- When you are ready to close the meditation, come back to a standing position with your weight equally distributed across both feet.
- Close your eyes. Take a few deep breaths. Open your eyes fully and raise your gaze up to anchor yourself fully back in the surroundings you are in.
- Spend a few moments reorienting yourself with your surroundings before drawing your meditation to a close with a stretch and a deep breath.

Restorative yoga practice

Restorative yoga is a delicious practice. You may have heard of yin yoga, which is a mostly floor-based practice where postures are held for 3–5 minutes. Restorative yoga deepens this practice a little further, with postures being held for anywhere up to 20 minutes.

The intention of a restorative yoga practice is to deepen and regulate the mind-body-soul connection, to release trapped energy or emotion held in the body and to regulate the nervous system. It is somewhere between movement and a traditionally still meditation practice. That being said, it can, at times, be super challenging. You might experience resistance or frustration while holding some poses, but this is all part of it. The practice requires us to meet our edges both physically and emotionally, and then to soften lovingly and surrender to it.

Restorative yoga can be practised at any time of day, but you might find it well placed as an evening activity during your self-led retreat.

You will need:

a yoga mat; cushions, bolsters and blankets; a candle (optional); incense (optional); a lighter or matches (optional); music (optional); a timer (optional); and an eye pillow (optional).

The practice

- Set up a comfortable nest on your yoga mat and create a soothing, relaxing space. Dim lights, light candles and burn delicious smells if you choose.
- Decide how long you would like to hold each posture for, from 5–20 minutes. You will need something to signal when time is up, like a song that is the length of time you have chosen, or a gentle alarm on your phone.
- Take your time transitioning between each pose. You might need to support your knees or take a pause between each pose. Listen to your body as you go.

The poses

Try these three restorative poses during your retreat:

1. Supported child's pose: On your yoga mat, sit back onto your feet with your knees out wide toward the edges of the mat. Place a bolster between your legs (so it's pointing to the top of your mat). Allow your body to rest forward onto the bolster with your head turned to one side and your arms resting on either side of the bolster. It might feel nice to place a blanket over your back. Turn your head halfway through the pose so that it is facing the other direction.

2. Reclined butterfly pose: Sit with your legs out straight in front of you. Place a bolster at the base of your spine, following the same direction as the long edges of your mat. Bring the soles of your feet together in front of you and allow your knees to fall out to the side (you might like to put a cushion under each knee). Rest your torso back onto the bolster, which should be supporting your spine, neck and head. Allow your arms to rest out wide so that your chest is open.

3. Legs up the wall: Place your yoga mat facing a wall and place a blanket over it. Lie flat on your back on your yoga mat and blanket. You might also like to place a blanket over your body too, and have an eye pillow within reaching distance. Wriggle your bottom down so that it is touching the wall. Swing your legs up so they are flat against the wall, as are the backs of your heels. The soles of your feet should be facing up toward the ceiling. Place your eye pillow over your eyes and rest here, breathing easy.

Expressive dance practice

Expressive dance is unchoreographed, uninhibited movement. It requires you to allow your body to move in any way that feels good without conscious direction. "Dancing like none is watching" is a lot easier when no one is watching (yay for self-led retreats!). Whether it's in a hotel room, your living room or outside of your shepherd's hut, moving your body in this way can feel like the ultimate reset.

So much tension is held in the body. As we explored in the "Validating emotions rituals" in Chapter Three (see Rituals and practices), repressed emotions can get blocked and stored in the body, manifesting as tension, pain or disease. The beauty of an expressive dance practice is that we don't need to concern ourselves too much with the story attached to these blocks, analysing or reflecting on it. Instead, we are just giving the energy or emotions attached to them an outlet to be released.

No matter how you are feeling, engaging in this practice, even just for one song, will guarantee an energy shift, feeling just that little bit lighter afterward. Some people are put off by the word "dance", so you can replace it with "movement" if it feels more freeing and inviting to you.

You will need:

music that will make you dance like no one is watching (optional).

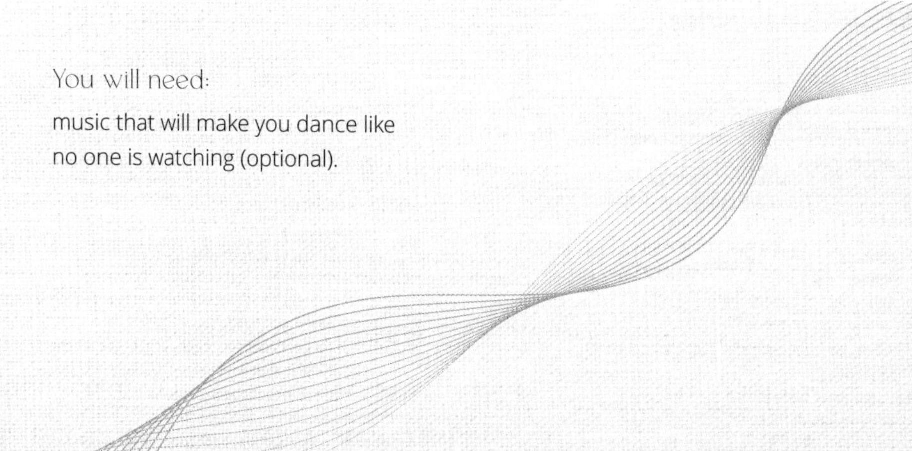

The practice

- You don't need music for this practice but it can certainly help. Find a song that makes you feel like moving your body. It might be an instrumental song, drumming or even your favourite pop song. As long as you like it and you can move your body to it.
- Start by taking a few deep breaths and checking in with your body, mind and soul. How are you feeling? How does your body feel? How is your heart?
- Press play on your chosen piece of music or soundtrack.
- Close your eyes and listen to the sounds around you. Start to allow your body to move on its own accord. You might like to start with a gentle sway back and forth or a rotation of the hips, head or wrists.
- Allow your body to move in whatever way feels good. You might find that you stretch, move closer to the ground, spin or shake. Nothing is off the table. This is your expressive movement, guided by the body itself. Nobody is watching, remember!
- Notice if any self-judgement creeps in: the voice of ego that might carry a self-critical tone, saying something like "What would people think if they saw me now!". Just acknowledge any resistance or judgement that comes up and stay connected to your body and movement.
- The beauty of this practice is there are no rules. Just move in a way that feels good to you. Something you might experience is smiling or laughing as you move. At other times tears might be released. Everything is welcome as a form of release and expression.
- When the track or playlist ends, or when you are ready to close the practice, come back to a standing position in stillness and check in with your body, mind and heart again. How does your body feel now? How does your heart feel?

Mindful sketching practice

Creativity and mindfulness are perfect companions. When engaged in a creative activity, time itself warps. One hour can feel like 10 minutes. The two complement each other so deeply it's hard to unpick which facilitates which. Is it our ability to be present that allows for a creative surge to express itself through us? Or is it engaging in a creative act that leads us into an ultra state of presence? I think both are true at the same time.

When we consider mindfulness alone, it's not just presence that is important, according to formal mindfulness practice. Jon Kabat-Zinn – a leader in the field of mindfulness and meditation – teaches that there are nine pillars of mindfulness, which allow us to graciously live in the present moment. These pillars are: patience, a beginner's mind, acceptance, gratitude, generosity, letting-go, surrender, non-judging and non-striving. Now imagine if we brought these attributes to a creative activity. We would be able to create freely for the purpose of expression. We might even see the creative act as a portal or doorway for the subconscious mind to express itself. So often, creativity is blocked by the thinking, judging mind. Often, we won't even let ourselves try for fear of failure, making a mess or not being good enough.

During your self-led retreat, you might wish to allow yourself to play with creativity throughout. Sketch or doodle by the fire or write a short story or poem while resting on a picnic bench in the park. When we are fearful of or detached from our creative essence it can be tricky to get started. The following practice should help get your creative juices flowing.

You will need:

your journal; a handful of pens, or paints and paint brushes; and a nature sounds playlist (optional).

The practice

- Grab your journal or some paper, and a handful of pens or paints.
- Set up a little creative station ideally in the great outdoors. If you are indoors, you may like to listen to a nature sounds playlist.
- Centre yourself by closing your eyes and taking a few deep breaths.
- Take your awareness to your ears and notice all the sounds around you. Without trying too much, just listen to the orchestra of sound of the ever-unfolding present moment.
- Pick up a pen or a paint brush and start to sketch what you can hear. This might be sketching little caricatures, doodles or literal or abstract representations of the sounds you are hearing.
- If you notice the thinking or critical mind creeping in, pause, take a breath and return your awareness to your ears and the sounds around you. Remember the pillars of mindfulness – particularly non-judgement, acceptance and surrender – and continue creating.
- Doodle, sketch or paint for as long as feels right.

Slow life practice

There is a famous Lao Tzu quote that says "Nature does not hurry, yet everything is accomplished". We can learn so much from the pace and beauty of the natural world, and the perfectly imperfect order of it all.

So often in life we are seeking to be in control and we are in such a hurry. We might convince ourselves of things like "If only I were further ahead, I would feel happy", or, "If only things would go exactly my way, I would feel peace". All the while, the natural world doesn't concern itself with such things.

The term and lifestyle practice "slow living" is widely used and adopted today. Or at least, there's a desire to embody the practice among many. The practice of slow living encourages people to do less, and instead do the things that really matter to them, with a greater state of presence and gratitude, savouring the experience of life at a slower pace rather than racing through it. This is an intention you can embody and start to practise throughout your self-led retreat, which can then be weaved into your daily life through an integration process (see Chapter Five: Integration). In fact, you can see the act of choosing to self-retreat as an embodiment of slow living in itself.

These slow living practices are so simple, but I often hear guests say when on a group retreat how powerful it is to be given permission to do them. Except here, on your self-led retreat, you will be giving yourself permission to embrace a slow life.

You will need:

a blanket or cushion (optional).

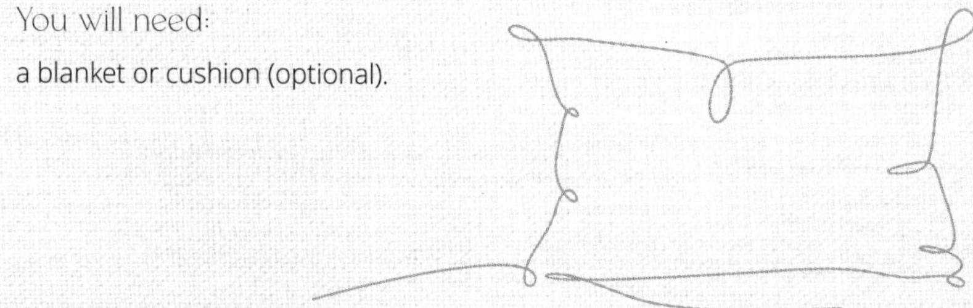

The practice

- Take yourself to a patch of earth. This might be in the garden, a field, a park, the forest floor or a beach.
- Position a blanket, cushion, or something that will help you spend some time comfortably on the ground. Make sure your phone is switched off and keep distractions of any kind – books, magazines or even your journal – in your bag.
- Come down to lie on the earth. This, quite simply, is going to be the main activity of this practice.
- Spend a few moments engaging your senses in turn. Spend five minutes noticing what you can see, from the obvious things to the tiniest little detail. Re-engage with the Lao Tzu saying "Nature does not hurry, yet everything is accomplished". Notice the movement of the wind through grass. The unfurling of a flower bud. The dance of sunlight on water. Watch nature as she moves and flows slowly at her own unhurried pace. Notice if, after a while, you take a few deep involuntary inhales or sighs. This is a sign your nervous system is regulating and is the state we are in when embodying slow living.
- Spend five minutes listening to the sounds and the space between sounds. Notice the silent pauses where sound seems to arise from and return to.
- Next, spend 10 minutes with your senses wide open. Notice the temperature on your skin, the sounds, smells, tastes and sights. Just giving yourself permission to be, nothing more, nothing less. In this practice, you are still, rested and present, witnessing nature, life and the world move around you. You are initiating a slower, more attuned pace of being.

Seasonal nature altar practice

Creating a nature altar is a way of honouring the reciprocal and interconnected relationship we have with nature. It can help remind us we are part of, not separate to, nature. It can also provide a focal point to remind us of our intentions, our hopes and dreams, and self and spiritual connection.

Altars might be synonymous with religious approaches, but they have been a prominent part of almost all ancient cultures across the world, including pagan practices. Connecting with the seasons teaches us so much about how to live, such as to see life as a cycle, to be present and to live in a state of non-resistance. Creating an altar in your retreat space is not only a mindful and creative activity, but it is a rich and deep spiritual activity too.

You may wish to do this practice on the first morning of your self-led retreat. If you're not at home for your self-retreat, you will simply dismantle your altar and give the items back to nature before you leave at the end of your retreat. These things are not meant to be permanent fixtures; they are meant to serve the purpose of honouring and then letting go when the time is right. The altar you will create as part of this practice is to honour the time and space you have taken for yourself on your self-led retreat. It will be a reminder of your retreat intention, and how letting it go at the end is a powerful part of the integration process (as you will find out in Chapter Five: Integration).

You will need:

a container to collect foraged items in; a candle; a lighter or matches; and any items from your tool kit that you'd like to include on your altar.

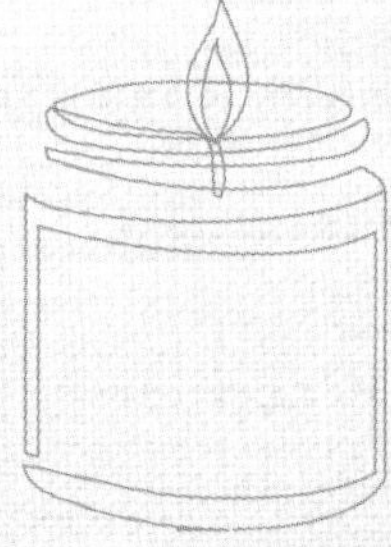

The practice

- Grab a container of some sort to collect foraged items in, be it a foraging basket or tote bag, and remind yourself of your retreat intention before you set off.
- Take yourself on a nature walk somewhere you feel called to visit. It might be your local beach, park or forest. Is there a location that complements your intention? It might even be a gentle stroll around the area you are in.
- As you head off on your walk with your intention in mind, forage for any items in nature that feel pleasing, speak to your intention or you feel called to include.
- Focus on quality not quantity. The items you forage – whether it's a shell, pine cone, feather or stone – should have meaning to you and your intention.
- When you return to your retreat setting, gather a candle and anything else from your tool kit that you think you would like to include in your altar, like photos or images.
- Light a candle in the centre of the space where you will create your altar (which should be somewhere prominent). It should be something you will see often to act as a frequent reminder of your intention. Let the arrangement of all the items you have collected or brought with you be a creative act. Savour and enjoy the process, reminding yourself of the significance of each item as it's placed. You might find you add to the altar as you engage in other activities throughout your retreat.
- Every time you see your altar, let it be a reminder of your intention, your divine connection to nature and your true essence within.
- At the end of your retreat, take some time to mindfully dismantle your altar, giving the parts that came from nature back to nature. Seasonal altars, whether created regularly at home or on retreat, remind us of the beauty of impermanence and our reciprocal relationship with the natural world.

Morning light and movement practice

There is a growing body of evidence to prove that exposing yourself to direct sunlight as soon as you wake up has enormous benefits. According to Andrew Huberman, getting 5–10 minutes of direct sunlight early in the morning helps to regulate your circadian clock – which helps you to stay awake and alert during the day and to sleep better at night – and aids the body to produce serotonin, a feel-good neurotransmitter that boosts a sense of happiness and calmness.

Moving your body first thing in the morning gets your circulation flowing, which activates the immune system. It also helps to produce endorphins, another feel-good hormone that is responsible for reducing stress, relieving pain and boosting mood. Combine direct sunlight early on and some morning movement, and you have a recipe for setting yourself up for a glorious retreat day.

The movement you choose during your retreat is completely up to you. But here is a practice to get you started, which focuses on circulation and flexibility.

You will need:

a glass of water (placed by your bedside the night before performing this ritual); and comfortable clothing (optional).

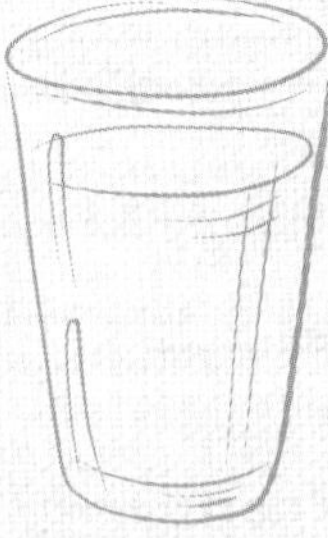

The practice

- As soon as you wake up in the morning, try not to hit snooze. Instead, gently swing your legs over the side of the bed. You are on retreat, remember, so an afternoon nap is absolutely possible later in the day!
- Take a few big sips of water before slowly standing up and putting on comfortable clothes to move your body in (or staying in your pjs).
- If you have access to a garden, walk outside barefoot. Otherwise, take your shoes off when you arrive at your chosen morning movement spot.
- Face the sunlight without sunglasses, but avoid staring directly into the sun.
- Stand tall with your feet directly on the earth, close your eyes for a moment and feel the morning light on your face. Take a deep breath.
- Open your eyes. With an inhale, reach your arms out wide and up to the sky. Imagine connecting with universal energy above – as if scooping it up with your arms and hands – before bringing your palms together above your head.
- With an exhale, draw your hands down to a prayer pose in front of your heart, as if drawing energy down into your body. Repeat this three times.
- Next, start to gently pat your chest with both hands. Move the patting motion around to the side of your ribs, your back (as far as you can reach), your stomach and lower back. Gently pat down the legs and shake each leg out in turn. Gently pat down each arm and then shake each arm out in turn.
- Roll your head gently from side to side and roll your shoulders. You might find intuitively you want to take a few stretches here.
- Check in with your body and notice what would feel good in the moment. Would adding the "Expressive dance practice" or the "Silent walking meditation practice" from Chapter Three (see Mindfulness, nature and movement practices) be nice here?
- When you feel ready to close, repeat the action of raising the arms up to the sky and drawing energy down to the body to close.

Preparing for sleep practice

The space and pace of a retreat allows for a bedtime routine to not only be sacred and unhurried, but to also be a practice of spiritual or self-connection.

The liminal state between wakefulness and being asleep is a mystical state, where the subconscious mind is open to influence and nourishment. Incorporating a nourishing bedtime into your self-led retreat will help seal in all the insights and benefits you've experienced throughout the day.

Preparing the body for sleep is an important step, and one that is often rushed. We will almost certainly brush our teeth and wash our face before bed, but the rest of the body, mind and soul is expected to just switch off without an intentional transition. Engaging the senses is a simple way to initiate one.

For this practice, you might like to do one or all of the following during the practice:

- Use diluted essential oils such as lavender, ylang ylang or clary sage on your pulse points or as a pillow spray.
- Mindfully sip mint tea without any distractions.
- Gently massage your shoulders, neck and hands.
- Dim the lights around two hours before bed or spend the evening in candlelight.
- Listen to classical or binaural beats music for sleep.

You will need:

a timer.

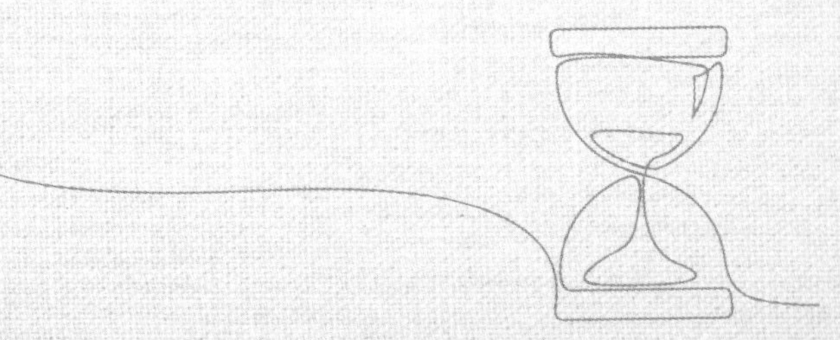

The practice

- Come to a seated position on the floor by your bed, with your legs stretched out in front of you and your back supported by the bed. Close your eyes and breathe evenly for a moment.
- Set a timer for five minutes. When you are ready, start to practise a breathing technique called 3-4-5. To practise, gently inhale to the count of three. Hold your breath to the count of four. Breath out slowly to the count of five. Continue doing this until the timer sounds.
- Set a timer again for a further five minutes and sit in quiet closed eye meditation. Focus on the flow of breath coming and going all by itself and the sensations of breath in your body. Notice if thoughts or images come and go (that's totally normal). Try to stay connected to your breath and the sensations in your body until the timer sounds.
- Come up to sit on the side of the bed and notice if your body wants you to stretch or twist before you get into bed. Honour whatever you find by moving your body in that way.
- Place your hands over your heart and spend a few moments reflecting on the day you've had, any insights you have experienced or any pleasure you have felt. Invite a feeling of gratitude to swell up from within the heart space and bring a gentle smile to your face.
- Say "Thank you" out loud to yourself and to the universe. This is a perfect opportunity for prayer if it feels right for you.
- Bring this feeling of gratitude, self-connection and universal connection with you and get into bed.
- Spend a few moments really noticing the comfort of being in bed. Consciously relax the muscles of the body before affirming to yourself silently "I give myself permission to rest and drift off into a deep and nourishing sleep".

Self-reflection exercises

Journalling is a powerful tool for self-reflection. It offers you an intimate, non-judgemental space to express yourself. I like to see my journal as my trusted companion, my wise counsel and my compassionate best friend who is always there to listen and receive. Through a journalling practice, we can clear through the weeds of the mind to identify and process our thoughts and emotions in a safe and contained way. The key is to practise self-compassion as you go and to write in an unedited fashion. Undo all you've been taught about writing to form or to impress. Journalling is a form of messy, raw self-expression, not a well crafted piece of writing that has to be perfect. It is an intimate conversation with yourself on a soul level.

Reconnect to your values journalling exercise

In order to live authentically, you must be living in line with your values. When something is aligned with our values, hopes and dreams we might feel energised, curious, peaceful or hopeful. When something is misaligned, we might experience the opposite: a lack of energy or feelings of unease.

Spending time on your self-led retreat reflecting on your values can give you a powerful foundation from which to uncover where you might be living out of alignment. The power of change first starts with awareness.

You might also like to pair this exercise with the "What lights you up journalling exercise" in Chapter Three (see Self-reflection exercises) as the two are innately intertwined.

You will need:

your journal and a pen; a candle; and a lighter or matches.

The exercise

- Grab your journal and pen and light a candle to signify the start of the exercise.

  Explore the following journalling questions:

  Who do you most admire? What are their qualities? How do they make you feel?

  When have you experienced envy? What is it that you envy? How does it make you feel?

  What do you love most about the way things currently are in your life?

  What do you see, feel or experience when you allow yourself to fantasise about things being different?

  When being a role model to others, what is important to you? What would you hope to model to others?

- Take a pause. Have a glass of water, take your gaze out the window for a few moments or take a few deep breaths, before returning to the reflective exercise.

- Take a look over what you have written and notice if there are any patterns or values that are jumping out at you. For example, "Living simply", "Being grateful" or "Being generous".

- Write out any values that feel like a safe anchor. These might change and refine as your retreat progresses or your reflective inner work deepens during and beyond your retreat.

- You can use these values as a filtering system when making a decision or choice. Run the decision through the filter of these values. Do they align? If you are trying to make a decision, you can explore this filtering practice in your journal as a continuation of this exercise.

What lights you up journalling exercise

I remember years ago feeling so detached from my sense of self and authenticity that I felt unenthused by most things. I had completely forgotten what lit me up, what I truly enjoyed or what brought me joy. We aren't able to be a light in the world unless we give ourselves permission to experience and embody what lights us up. "Giving ourselves permission" is something that comes up a lot when exploring self-care and authentic living, whether it's giving ourselves permission to experience joy, pleasure, hope, creativity, self-expression, connection or love.

Often, the biggest block to allowing ourselves to experience such things is a lack of self-worth. In fact, when we embark on a self-reflective journey and "do the work", more often than not we can trace a great deal of our stumbling blocks back to a lack of worth. Rediscovering what lights you up requires you to engage in the process with a childlike sense of curiosity, and to bring playfulness back into your life.

Following what lights you up in life is like following a breadcrumb trail to authenticity. So often self-reflection and healing requires trudging through the murky stuff and bringing light into the shadows within ourselves. But it doesn't always have to involve this. Reconnecting with what lights you up is an exercise of reigniting lights within that might just have gone out. Perhaps it will feel right to imagine the process of finding those lights to be like a great game of hide and seek.

You will need:

your journal and a pen; a candle; and a lighter or matches.

The exercise

- Grab your journal and a pen and light a candle to signify the start of the exercise.

    Start by exploring the following journalling questions:

    What activities did you enjoy as a child?

    When was the last time you belly laughed? Or laughed until you cried?

    When have you felt proud?

    What section of a book shop do you head to first?

    When have you felt most "yourself"?

    If you won the lottery, what would you do?

    What simple things bring you pleasure or joy in your day-to-day life?

- Take a pause and reflect on what you have written. Allow yourself to journal as an unedited stream of consciousness about what has come up in your reflections above.
- Is what lights you up becoming clear? If so, write out or doodle a few things on a separate page in your journal under the title "What lights me up".

Writing poetry from within exercise

As discussed in Chapter Three (see Readings), poetry can be medicine and meditation. Reading poems can have a visceral effect if they resonate deeply with us, just as a piece of art or a song can. Poems can touch us so deeply sometimes that tears form or a sense of inner surrender occurs. Writing poetry can also be a potent form of self-expression and it can also alchemise and process feelings.

Myself and a lot of people I have coached all seem to experience a similar thing where a poem just seems to arrive. It bubbles up from somewhere deep within and it's often a challenge to catch it by writing it down before it's flown off again. When I am captivated by the present moment, in love with life or being radically honest with myself about how I'm feeling, it somehow unlocks a door within me and a poem surges forth. If you invite that same creative surge into your experience, you may find that during the peace and space of your retreat you experience something similar. So often we block that flow because of preconceived ideas about what a poem is, or that we're not creative. But poems don't need to rhyme or be written to form. They are merely rhythmic expressions of truth.

To oil the hinges of the door that blocks the flow of words freely flowing from deep within you, try the following exercise during your retreat.

You will need:

your journal and a pen.

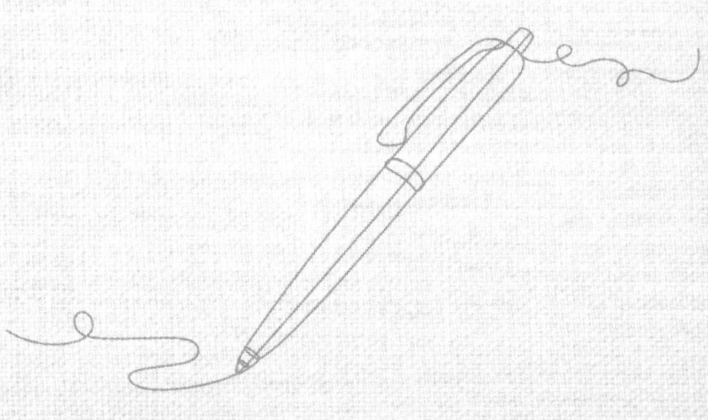

The exercise

- Bring an emotion to mind and write down what colour you associate with that emotion.
- On the next line, write down what might that emotion taste like.
- On the next line, write down what might it sound like.
- On the next line, write down what texture is it.
- On the next line, write down what weather you associate with it.
- On the next line, write down what in nature might represent that emotion.
- Come back to the first line (the colour) and expand on it, giving it more detail. What shade is it? Is there an object the same colour as it? Do this for each line, adding more description to it.
- Spend a few moments editing what you have written without overediting or getting caught up in the detail. Just shape different lines and words so that it feels pleasing.
- When you have finished, title your poem by the emotion and write it out neatly on a page in your journal.

Rewrite your script affirmation exercise

Each of us has an inner belief system that operates just outside of our conscious awareness. Our subconscious programming directs our lives whether we like it or not. This programming is made evident in repeating patterns or circumstances, habits, reactions, actions and emotions that keep showing up for us in our lives. Working with the subconscious is a wild and brave journey to undertake, but ultimately, without self-knowledge and self-awareness, it is near impossible to redirect our lives in a direction of travel we truly want to go in without tripping over the same old stumbling blocks, or finding ourselves right back where we started. Same stuff, different situation.

We cannot manifest a new reality without becoming familiar with the deeper held beliefs about the world, others and self. In the safe space of your self-led retreat, this practice can be a gentle way to become aware of and reprogramme some unwanted unconscious beliefs. It may also be the gateway to seeking further support from trained therapists to help dive deeper into this area of healing on the other side of your retreat.

You will need:

your journal and a pen.

The exercise

- Bring to mind a time when you felt triggered, and your body physically reacted to an external stimulus by going into fight, flight or freeze mode. Perhaps when an emotional nerve was poked and you emotionally reacted in some way, losing your balance and perhaps lashing out or shutting down.
- Write down in your journal what happened and how it felt in that moment. Think "They did this", and "I said that".
- Then write down what was happening internally for you. What was happening in your body? How did your nervous system react?
- Take your time with the next part, but start to investigate on the page what inner beliefs you might have about yourself, others or the world, which might have led you to react in the way you did.
- Draw a line down the middle of a page in your journal. In the left-hand column, write out any negative beliefs you uncover as statements. For example, "I am not welcome", "It is not safe to express my feelings" or "I can't trust people".
- Take a breath.
- In the right-hand column, rewrite the beliefs as positive beliefs. For example, "I am welcome", "It is safe to express my feelings" or "I trust people".
- Read down through the column of negative beliefs and notice how it feels in the body. Notice what vibration of energy you are embodying while reading these beliefs. Then read through the list of positive beliefs and notice the energy shift. How might it feel to truly believe and embody these beliefs? What might you attract? How might life feel different?
- Then (and this might feel cringey at first) get out your phone and record yourself saying the positive beliefs list out loud, repeating the list three times.
- Close your eyes and listen back to the new beliefs. Do this at various times throughout your retreat, and in the weeks and months following as part of your integration stage in Chapter Five.

Deep gratitude journalling exercise

Gratitude is such a simple practice that it often gets overlooked or not taken seriously. This practice is a delicious practice to incorporate into a self-led retreat, as it leaves you feeling topped up, empowered and full of life.

It's interesting to note that the typical human programming is wired to have a slightly negative bias, which leads us to not only focus more heavily on the negative things, but also to internalise negative experiences more deeply, overanalysing or overthinking them. This is thanks to the ancient part of our brain that is wired to be more astutely aware of threat and danger in order to keep us safe. Without conscious awareness, this negative bias can run riot in our lives, leaving us feeling depleted, unmotivated and depressed. Any gratitude practice involves consciously bringing to mind the things in our lives that we are grateful for.

No matter how much of a grip that negative bias has over our experience, there is always something to be grateful for. Expressing our gratitude in some way amplifies the feeling and focus of gratitude. It manifests the feeling into our tangible reality and makes it hard not to believe. As the saying goes, "Happiness is only real when shared". Could the same be said for love and gratitude?

You will need:

a journal and a range of different coloured pens.

The exercise

- On a fresh page in your journal write the word "gratitude" in the middle of the page and circle it. Make it bold and beautiful.
- Close your eyes and take a few centring breaths. Connect with your heart space and heart energy. Bring to mind a few things that you are grateful for.
- Write them out, dotted around the page. See if you can jot down at least 20 things.
- Underneath each thing you are grateful for, in a different coloured pen, write out how that thing makes you feel. For example, loved, seen, supported, safe, hopeful.
- Notice which of the things you are grateful for carries the most energetic charge for you. What is lighting you up as you reflect on it? What carries a strong, positive emotional charge? Highlight these things in some way by circling them or putting an illustration next to them.
- Write these intense "gratitudes" out on a fresh page in your journal and reflect on how you can show your appreciation for these things. If it's a person, you could write them a letter or a card. If it's a place, you could take an offering with you next time you return. If it's an opportunity you've been given, how could you give back in some way?
- Play around with ideas. Are you able to action any of these things during your retreat, like writing a letter of thanks and love? If not, make yourself a plan for expressing your gratitude as part of your integration stage (see Chapter Five).

Lining up the starting blocks direction planning exercise

Much like you practised at the start of this book, getting clear on what you need for your retreat and getting clear on what you need and want from life is the first step to change, whether that's internal or external change.

Change is nothing to be frightened of; it is one of the few certainties in life. Another certainty is that we are not in control; life always seems to have its own plan. We can, however, decide which course to take, and how we respond to life and change, when it comes. It takes a balance of clarity, direction and action, and surrender. A teacher of mine would always say to me "100 per cent intention, 100 per cent surrender".

Intention setting is lining up the starting blocks. It is consciously choosing the direction of travel we wish to move in, and a direction aligned with your values (see the "Reconnect to your values journalling exercise" earlier in this section), desires, hope and dreams. Getting clear on this direction of travel is the first step. The second, very vital step is taking action of some kind.

You might like to pair this self-reflective exercise with the following "Taking action exercise" as the two complement each other perfectly. This exercise can also be used as a regular check in. It is something I do yearly or every couple of years, allowing life to have its own way with me but ensuring I take my rightful seat as a co-pilot working with life.

You will need:

a journal and a pen.

The exercise

Something you might like to try before taking this self-reflection exercise to the page is to take a walk and ponder on the question: what is my intention for life at the moment? Turn your phone onto airplane mode to avoid any digital distractions and allow your mind to wander and dream as you ponder where you currently are and where you would like to go in life. Walking is a brilliant form of exercise that also helps with mental clarity. So take the question "What do I want?" for a walk. When you return, take to your journal to explore the following journalling prompts:

- Are your starting blocks currently lined up in the direction of travel you would like to go in? How does it feel?
- What is blocking the path?
- What adjustments could you make now or in the near future?
- How do you feel about surrender? Is it something you are currently doing?
- What would 100 per cent intention, 100 per cent surrender look like for you right now?
- What support do you need?
- What affirmation would support this new direction?

Taking action exercise

So often talent, creativity, love and opportunities pass people by because they don't take action, say yes or lean fully into what they truly want. It feels safer to stay in the shadows and to not try. "Comfort zone" has the word "comfort" in it for a reason. However, sometimes this stagnation can lead to a victim mentality state where we might believe – and tell just about anyone who'll listen – how the world is against us, nothing goes our way and other people seem to get all the luck. This is often a mistake made with a manifesting practice too. People can mistake that all they need to do is to wish for something and it will manifest in their lives, but that's not the way life, or the laws of the universe, work.

We must be clear on what we want but we must also then take action toward it. This doesn't mean creating ourselves mountains to climb or setting unachievable goals; it means to make small steps and make habit and belief changes to align with what it is we want to bring about. We must also feel what it is like to be the change we wish to bring about. We must take responsibility, remain conscious and present and respond authentically to life as it unfolds.

You will need:

your journal and a pen. You will also need to have completed the "Lining up the starting blocks direction planning exercise" before beginning this practice.

The exercise

- Take a moment to skim-read over your reflections from the "Lining up the starting blocks direction planning exercise". How does it make you feel rereading what you have written? What themes surface for you? What is the tone of your reflections? Hopeful, confidence, nervous? What clearly comes through as your desires and intentions?
- Choose one or two things from your reflections above that you wish to work with. Write them out clearly on the page.
- Reflect, through journalling, on what physical actions and baby steps you could take to start the energy moving in your chosen direction of travel.
- Reflect through journalling what daily habits help or hinder this progress.
- Reflect through journalling what affirmations would support your progress.
- On a fresh new page, write out three steps or actions you are going to take, a daily habit you are going to start/stop/continue, and three affirmations as "I am" statements to help keep the energy moving in your chosen direction of travel. For example, "I am going to reach out to [insert name] to ask for help", "I am going to start each morning revisiting my intention", "I am going to integrate a five minute meditation into my morning routine" or "I am worthy of a life I love".

Authentic self journalling exercise

Your authentic or higher self isn't something separate from you; you are already them. There is a part of you who is always plugged in. A wise, all-knowing part of you that knows what to do and when. It isn't some version of yourself you might be in the future. Time and space don't exist in this mystical realm.

The information this tuned in version of you can receive is widely debated. Some believe this part of you is channelled from a higher source or universal energy. Some believe in ancestral spirits or spirit guides. Some believe it's all a load of nonsense. But the intriguing things about the mystical realm is nothing can be proved either way. Whatever feels right and true for you might feel very different to me and perhaps that is the way it is supposed to be. The mystery then remains just that.

One thing I do believe is that you don't need to work harder or prove yourself in any way in order to be your authentic self. In fact, it requires the opposite. It requires surrender, again, into being. When we are ultra present and open, captivated by the present moment and are self-aware, we are more able to receive guidance from our higher self, or channel it from a universal energy.

You will need:

your journal and a pen.

The exercise

- Take a few centering deep breaths before you begin this journalling exercise.
- Start to write out a scene as if you are in it in real time, allowing yourself to feel how it would feel if it were real in this very moment. Imagine you have just woken up in the most perfect place. Describe every little detail on the page. What is the room like, what does it smell like, where is it? How do the sheets feel against your skin? Is anyone else there? What can you see out of the window or door?
- Next, write out what you would do on your perfect day. What does your perfect morning look like? How do you feel? What are you wearing? How do you look in the mirror? What activities do you engage with? What do you eat for lunch? Allow your imagination to run wild and bring up a vivid image of this perfect day as you write.
- Allow this journalled visualisation to continue throughout the day and evening until you return to your bed.
- When you have finished the exercise, take a deep breath and allow yourself to marinate in the feelings the visualisation conjured up. Imagine this image of you and the feeling you are feeling right now being beamed out into the universe as a hologram.

Boundaries journalling exercise

When we're able to embody our authentic self and confidence, setting and maintaining healthy boundaries becomes a lot easier. In fact, without the skill of being comfortable with boundaries, it is almost impossible to truly be authentic. I came across a powerful definition of boundaries once that stuck with me. It was that setting boundaries teaches people how to love us. It flipped everything I thought I knew about boundaries on its head.

I'd always interpreted "boundaries" as purely self-preservation, keeping people out. But setting a boundary just means communicating your needs and preferences clearly to others. If they don't know, how can we expect them to comply? It can also mean being clear within ourselves of what is and isn't tolerable for us, and saying yes or no in accordance without guilt. For example, if a person in your life is particularly draining, a boundary you might set for yourself is to only see them once a month, or to say no to what you want to say no to.

Setting boundaries is self-protective, but it is also loving. When we don't have clear boundaries in place we run the risk of being taken advantage of, giving too much of ourselves to something or someone, or not being true to ourselves. Those of us who struggle with co-dependency or people pleasing might struggle with setting boundaries. But remember, awareness is the first step to change.

You will need:

your journal and a pen.

The exercise

Implementing healthy boundaries is only possible when you are aware of your relationship with boundaries. However, becoming aware of this relationship may take some time and patience. Spend some time in quiet reflection during your retreat journalling your answers to the prompts found below. You may like to return to this exercise at a later date to revisit these questions as part of an ongoing integration process in your daily life.

- What are your beliefs about boundaries?
- What is your relationship to setting boundaries? Do you find it difficult or easy to identify and communicate them?
- How does it feel when someone else sets a boundary with you?
- How does it feel when a boundary of yours has been crossed?
- What do healthy physical and emotional boundaries look like for you?
- How might you communicate this clearly to others?
- What boundaries surrounding your time and energy might serve you and your life? Who would you need to communicate this with?
- What support might you need?

Self-acceptance journalling exercise

Self-acceptance is an elusive pursuit for so many. It is the ability to look in the mirror and say "I love you, I forgive you, I accept you exactly as you are", and to really mean it.

Is authentic, intentional living possible without self-acceptance? Is the ability to truly love another possible without loving ourselves first? Can a sense of purpose, achievement and contentment be possible if we don't love and accept ourselves for who we are? I don't believe self-acceptance leads to stagnation or letting ourselves off the hook. It is certainly the opposite to arrogance or an ego driven sense of self-importance or entitlement. We can only accept ourselves when we do face our shortcomings and take responsibility for them. There is a calmness and an openness to those who I have met who have mastered the art of self-acceptance. It feels safe and steady to be in their presence. It allows me to be more truthful and open. Self-acceptance is therefore not only a gift to ourselves and the lives we lead but it is also a gift to others.

There will be times in your life when you have felt in alignment, when your higher or authentic self has shown up and it felt good to be you. And there will undoubtedly be times when you felt a sense of misalignment, unease or even shame. Self-acceptance is not being perfect and always getting it right. It is about taking responsibility for ourselves on our individual evolutionary path to becoming more of who we truly are, understanding that we all make mistakes sometimes and that's ok. It is to know deeply this life is a gift and to say thank you for it all.

You will need:

your journal and a pen.

The exercise

For some it can feel uncomfortable, almost boastful, to bring to mind the things that we are proud of about ourselves or that we value in ourselves. This kind of conditioning keeps us small and in a loop of self-criticism. Take some time during your retreat to reflect on the following journalling prompts. Notice what it brings up for you and be kind to yourself, as you would to another.

- What are you most proud of?
- When has your authentic/highest self shown up? How did this feel? What did you do?
- What are you most grateful for about your body?
- What qualities do people comment on or thank you for?
- What part of yourself can you finally forgive, love, accept and integrate?
- What do you wish you believed about yourself? What positive affirmations might these sound like? Write these affirmations out clearly on a fresh page in your journal or on sticky notes and affirm them often to yourself.

Bringing it all together

The final part of this stage of planning your self-led retreat is to write out a schedule. This might sound a little dull or over-the-top, but it will help you stay focused and present during the retreat itself. Pick a few of the practices, rituals, exercises or readings that you wish to include in your retreat, and be sure to leave plenty of space for going with the flow, reading or napping too.

Turn this final piece of planning into a creative practice. Write your schedule out beautifully, as having one helps to turn the experience from being some nice, chilled time spent at a home or away space into a retreat. Remember, you are the guest of honour in this experience! If you were designing a retreat for your idol, you would likely spend time on the finer details, such as displaying a schedule for them so they know what's happening when. Why not do it for yourself too?

Checklist

Having worked through this chapter you should now have the following in place:

- ☐ A list of practices, rituals, readings or self-reflective exercises you would like to include in your retreat
- ☐ A retreat schedule, written out

Chapter Four

Your retreat

Your retreat is finally here! You have carefully planned and curated the very best experience for yourself. You have your tool kit to hand; a schedule ready to display; nourishing retreat meals and snacks to be enjoyed and savoured; and you have this book to support you through the very best bit: completely immersing yourself in the experience.

This chapter will guide you through getting set up once you've arrived at your venue, or are transitioning into your retreat experience at home. Let this stage of your retreat be slow, intentional and pleasurable. You deserve this.

Getting set up on retreat day

After you have arrived at your chosen retreat venue, getting yourself set up is a ritual in itself. It is all part of the process. When I'm leading group retreats this is the part where I'll prepare the spaces we will be using with candles and flowers. I might set up yoga mats and blankets in the meditation space; dot goodie bags and dressing gowns around the bedrooms; set the table; adjust the lighting; spritz rooms with essential oil spray; and hide little notes or affirmation cards in dressing gown pockets or on bathroom mirrors before preparing myself for the arrival of guests.

After I've set everything up, there is a transitional half an hour or so before guests start to arrive. A pause. I often make myself a cup of tea and sit in a window seat that has a view down the long drive of a venue I use regularly so that I can spot the first car as it approaches. This pause is when everything shifts, as I shift from planner to host and drop my energy from my head to my heart. I transition into handing myself over to the experience, however it may unfold. This is something I've brought into my self-led retreats as an initiation practice. A simple yet inaugural pause before the retreat begins.

This pause is something I recommend you do on your self-led retreat too. When you arrive at the venue, or the time has come to transition from the everyday into a retreat at home, take your time to set up, just as you might if you were holding space for a group retreat for others.

This might include:

- Setting up a meditation, yoga or movement space.
- Laying out your tool kit.
- Setting up your altar.
- Displaying flowers, candles, crystals or any such items around the space.
- Laying the table for your first meal.
- Having a shower or freshening up.
- Setting up a writing station for any journalling exercises you intend to engage with.
- Displaying your schedule somewhere.
- Cleansing the space with essential oil spritz, sage, incense or palo santo.
- Familiarising yourself with the garden or outdoor space.
- Displaying toiletries like they might at a spa in the bathroom.

This transition from everyday into retreat mode requires some or all of the above to be performed. If you wish to see your retreat as sacred time and space it should be treated as such, with tenderness, presence and care, just as you will be treating yourself during this time.

Another final yet essential step is preparing your people for your time away. What this means is letting the people closest to you know what you are doing,

where you are and asking them to give you space, especially if you are holding your retreat at home.

Something else I consider essential is including a digital detox as part of your retreat. Turn your phone off completely so there is no temptation to check the weather, the news, the group chat, social media, or to see if someone replied to your email. You can still keep your phone near you or on you if you're out for a walk (but just turned off or on airplane mode) if it facilitates a sense of safety during the retreat, so that you can really let go and fully immerse yourself in the experience. I also highly recommend including TVs, laptops and tablets in your retreat digital detox as well, but of course, it is entirely up to you. If you do decide to watch something as part of your retreat, consciously choose it. There are some support suggestions for dealing with resistance that comes up during digital detox in the next section in "Struggling with digital detox" later in this chapter.

Once you are all set up, allow yourself the simple, inaugural pause I mentioned earlier before initiating the start of your retreat with a simple opening ceremony (see the "Retreat opening ceremony" in Chapter Three – Rituals and practices). You might sit in the garden or by the fire with a cup of tea for a few moments, anchoring yourself into the present moment by engaging your senses. You are on retreat now! You so deserve this time.

Handing yourself over to the experience

It's time to cross the threshold and immerse yourself in the retreat experience. Enjoy and savour every second of it.

You may find that you sink into the flow of things immediately, or you may find it takes a little while to land. Just notice what is present for you, as an ongoing, fluid, living enquiry throughout your retreat experience. There may be times when you hit some resistance or blocks, and that's ok. This book will be here with you and for you throughout the retreat, and is something you can turn to for guidance during those times. Should you feel the need to be guided or supported through any resistance or challenge, turn to the coming pages to help you navigate your way through. A self-led retreat requires you to self-lead. This might take a little practice but it is a skill that is invaluable in daily life too. Be sure to turn to Chapter Five on the very last day before your retreat ends to work through how you will integrate any insights and learnings into daily life.

Now, it's time to dive into your retreat. Savour and enjoy every moment. Follow your schedule but allow room for changing course depending on how the retreat unfolds. Go slow, take a deep, satisfying breath and get stuck in.

Support pages for during your retreat

Meeting resistance or blocks during your retreat isn't a bad thing. In fact, we can choose to see them as useful information in our self-reflective journey.

If and when you uncover a block, choose to see it as a signpost to what needs healing, attention or love. See if you can adopt a "how curious" attitude to any resistance that comes up for you. Rather than getting consumed by the resistance, explore what is happening for you on the page through journalling. You might find an ah-ha moment or a nugget of gold hidden beneath it.

Here are some common themes that can crop up during a self-led retreat and some suggestions of how to work through or work with them.

Struggling to self-lead

By embarking on a self-led retreat, you are already becoming practised and competent in self-leading. The time, space and self-reflection available to you thanks to your conscious choice of taking a retreat will allow a deeper connection to your sense of self. But when we're not used to having the space and time for self-reflection, it can sometimes feel a little overwhelming.

If you find yourself feeling a little lost during your retreat, take a pause. Let all the effort go and have a breather. Your retreat should feel like nourishment, not "work". Start by acknowledging and validating your feelings, and return to the question "What do I need?" (or or revisit the "What do I need most?" section in Chapter Two: Planning your retreat). By validating your feelings and honouring them, you are self-leading!

One vitally important element of self-leadership is knowing when to ask for help, and actioning this need by reaching out. There is a difference between self-leading and self-reliance. Being in relationship with others is part of being human. Co-regulating, creating and communing in some way is essential for our survival and ability to thrive. It's not creating yourself a fortress and relying only on yourself. Self-leading is taking responsibility for yourself, taking loving action and empowering yourself with self-knowledge and resilience. You are here! You are already doing it. So reaching out to someone you value, love and trust – this might be a partner, friend, therapist or coach – during your retreat if you need to is also self-leading.

You might like to try:

from Chapter Three, the "Lining up the starting blocks direction planning exercise" (see Self-reflection exercises) or reading "The middle way" (see Readings).

Struggling with a digital detox

Never before in history have humans had a relationship with technology the way we do today. For 300,000 years our ancestors lived vastly different lives to the ones we live in the modern world. For the first time, we have digital gadgets attached to us 24 hours a day, seven days a week. The benefits of this are obvious on the surface, but the cost of this on our long-term mental health and wellbeing is still to be determined.

Phone addiction has been linked to increased levels of anxiety, agitation, depression and disorientation. Reaching for our phones is often the first thing we do in the morning and the last thing we do at night, so going cold turkey and taking a digital detox can bring up all sorts of things for people. Realising the impulsive reflex to reach for your phone even though it is off might be a little alarming, and it might bring up a sense of shame.

Be kind to yourself if you are experiencing any challenge around a digital detox during your retreat. See this as a mindful practice in itself. Notice when the urge to reach is there, bring your awareness back to the present moment by engaging your senses, and refocus on something nourishing. You might even thank that urge to reach for your phone, as it was the sign that your mind had slipped away from the present moment and fallen unconscious. Remind yourself that taking time away from digital distractions allows a deeper level of presence with yourself, which is the very reason you are here on retreat.

You might like to try:

from Chapter Three, the "Mindful sketching practice" (see Mindfulness, nature and movement practices) or "Reconnect to your values journalling exercise" (see Self-reflection exercise.

Feeling resistance to slowing down

When we shift gear from a busy, hectic life it can be a real challenge to slow down and focus on ourselves. I see it often for guests on group retreats, so go gently with yourself.

First, acknowledge and validate how you are feeling. When we are living constantly in a state of go, go, go, our nervous system is activated and on high alert, and we are in fight or flight mode. It can be a challenge for some who are so used to operating in this way to switch modes and to trust the safety of rest, space and quiet.

Get curious about what is going on for you. Ask yourself: is this a mental, emotional or physical sense of resistance to slowing down and resting? If it is mental, your internal narrative might sound something like "This is lazy" or "I'm bored". If it is emotional, it might manifest as a feeling of unease or loneliness. If it is physical, it might express itself as restless leg syndrome or fidgeting. Notice what is present for you and then remind yourself of your retreat intention. Remember, it may take a while to settle in. If it feels this way, it is completely normal. See it as a steady transition rather than an immediate switch we can press from one state to another.

You might like to try:

from Chapter Three, the "Slow life practice" (see Mindfulness, nature and movement practices) or "Rewrite your script affirmation exercise" (see Self-reflection exercises) or reading "Divine feminine rising" (see Readings).

Struggling with mindfulness

There are circumstances where mindfulness – bringing your conscious awareness to the present moment and becoming aware of what is present for you – can be overwhelming when paired with trauma. Although mindfulness-based approaches are widely used to treat trauma responses – such as post-traumatic stress – in acute cases, mindfulness can actually trigger traumatic symptoms, such as anxiety. If acute feelings of unease arise for you, reach out for help to a family member or friend, or a helpline service. This is certainly a situation where breaking a digital detox – if you are participating in one – is necessary.

You might like to try:

from Chapter Three, the "Body love ritual" (see Rituals and practices) or reading "It's going to be ok" (see Readings).

Feeling down during your retreat

The shadow self is the part of us that resides in our subconscious mind, out of conscious awareness. It can be the stuff we do not want to face, such as things we've long buried, are ashamed of, or are frightened of, including emotions, desires, memories and fears.

Shadow work is the term given to working through that stuff and bringing the light of our awareness into the darkness of our shadow in order to integrate it into our whole being. Shadow work is a delicate but powerful process. The idea is that all that repressed stuff is there whether we face it or not, but that by bringing light to it, we can start to process, heal, forgive or let go, allowing an inner sense of freedom, strength and wholeness on the other side.

Sometimes, shadow work is something we consciously embark on, choosing to venture into the dark. Other times, it is thrust upon us by life or circumstance. You will inevitably meet your shadow at times during your retreat. Either way, anchoring yourself in the safety of the present moment at regular points throughout your retreat can tether you to a sense of comfort and security. Don't be frightened of tears, instead, welcome them. They are a physical, emotional and energetic release.

You might like to try:

from Chapter Three, the "Validating emotions rituals" (see Rituals and practices) or reading "Dark night" (see Readings).

Resisting participating in the experience

This one can manifest in a number of sneaky little ways. I remember a guest on retreat some time ago really struggled to hand herself over to the experience. We went for a 20-minute silent group walk one afternoon and her resistance to the silence was so strong she simply couldn't participate. She spoke to others; hummed and commentated her way through the walk; proudly claimed that no one could tell her what to do and that she didn't see the point in the exercise; and was proud of her choice to not participate.

The ego's voice – the voice of fear – is so convincing sometimes. The ego fears change and the unknown, and it loves to make itself right. When in the grips of the ego, we are unable to soften and open to new experiences. It keeps us "self" focused and cuts us off from our intuition or ability to feel spiritually connected to nature or much else outside of ourselves. The ego isn't to be hated or damned, though. It is the part of us that is just trying to keep us safe. There is a famous Alan Watts quote that says "The biggest ego trip is to try and get rid of the ego". Instead, we can befriend that part of ourselves, call it in closer and listen to what it has to say. In doing so you might notice that it dissipates, eases or vanishes altogether. Just notice what is coming up for you and journal your thoughts out on the page.

You might like to try:

from Chapter Three, the "Expressive dance practice" (see Mindfulness, nature and movement practices) or reading "The search" (see Readings).

Worrying about going back to "real life" after your retreat

Sometimes a retreat can feel so good that we don't want to leave. I remember coming to the end of a weekend retreat I had attended and I experienced a surge of worry flooding through me at the thought of all I had to go back to. I had stepped off the treadmill and felt the anticipation of returning to immediate stress as soon as I returned, as if the treadmill itself had kept going and I had to hop straight back on at the same speed.

The antidote to this feeling is to remember your retreat is a journey and a transition, and to ensure the vital step of integration is factored into your retreat experience. This is covered in depth in Chapter Five: Integration. If you experience flashes of worry about the retreat coming to an end when you are nowhere near the end of the retreat, refamiliarise yourself with the present moment. Stay in the experience that is happening right now rather than losing yourself in the future. If it is nearing the end of your retreat, turn to Chapter Five and start working through the integration stage of your retreat, as this will extend way past the experience itself.

You might like to try:

from Chapter Three, the "Ritual bath" or "Ritual foot soak" (see Rituals and practices) or reading "Be here now" (see Readings).

Chapter Five

Integration

Integration is an essential part of a retreat. The reason we retreat is to gain perspective, reconnect or to top ourselves up. A retreat won't have a lasting impact on your life without incorporating a focus on integration into it. The retreat itself won't change your life, you will.

During the self-reflective space a retreat offers, you might have reconnected to your own inner wisdom and guidance system, but it's what happens from here after the retreat is over that really matters. As your retreat draws to a close it's time to ring the juice out of it, to get crystal clear on any insights you may have uncovered and to initiate an integration process to ensure you are able to embody and live out these learnings into your daily life.

Before you bring your retreat to a close,
turn your awareness to integration.

What is integration?

"Integration" is a term and process used and recognised in a number of spiritual, healing and psychological modalities, notably Eastern philosophies and Jungian psychology. In a healing sense, integration is the process of becoming whole. In Jungian psychology, it is used to describe the recognition and acceptance of all parts of our self and psyche. In Eastern philosophy, it often refers to the integration of spirituality within our daily lives. In the retreat context, integration involves a combination of all those things.

Without a focus on integration, a retreat becomes tokenistic. It's a nice thing to do but it doesn't have a great deal of impact for us in the long term. The real work comes when we return to "real life" and get to practise putting these learnings into practice. This is nothing to be daunted by or feared. For me, this is the most exciting and juicy part!

Focusing on integration reminds us that life is a glorious gift and every experience is an opportunity for learning and evolution. Life's experiences might not always be to our choosing, but each offers us an opportunity to get to know ourselves better and explore what it means to be human, to live and love more deeply and to become more of who we really are. The sacred pause offered through a self-led retreat gives me fuel, perspective, clarity and a sense of gumption so that, by the end, I look forward to going back to daily life and embodying all I have uncovered during my retreat – with varying levels of success.

There are many creative, practical and playful ways to integrate aspects of your retreat into daily life. The most important one might be to continue treating yourself like the guest of honour in your own life, as this is how we maintain self-care. This might mean to consider what food you put in your body, or to continue practising mindfulness, kindness and compassion to self. It might be to slow down, to choose nourishing activities for yourself, or to bring a curious beginner's mind to your daily life, not just the retreat experience. Or, it might be to embed a journalling practice or creative activities into daily life. All these things can be anchored in intention, and this is how we initiate the integration process.

Integration journalling exercise

The last reflection piece you might choose to do as part of your retreat is to initiate this integration stage and spend some time reflecting on the learnings or insights that have surfaced for you during the retreat. These insights might be obvious immediately, or need a little investigation.

Set up a beautiful writing station one last time. You might choose to make yourself a delicious beverage to have with you, or practise the "Heart-opening cacao ritual" from Chapter Three (see Rituals and practices) before you begin. See this last reflection as an act of self-care and self-leadership.

You will need:

a candle; a lighter or matches; beautiful music; and your journal and a pen.

The exercise

Grab your journal and take your time to look back over all you have scribbled down in it during your retreat experience. You can read through it word for word, or skim-read what you have written. See if any patterns surface in your reflections, and highlight or circle any key ah-ha moments or bits of wisdom that came through in your reflections. Notice how reading through your reflections makes you feel.

Next, reflect on these following questions:

- What did you enjoy most about this retreat experience?
- What did you find most challenging?
- What practices felt most nourishing or impactful? Why?
- What is your intention going forward?
- What do you need to do to stay anchored to this intention? What practices could you bring into daily life?
- What support do you need moving forward?
- What is the biggest insight or lesson you have uncovered during your retreat about yourself and your life?
- What are you most looking forward to about going back to "real life"?
- What would embodying all you have learned and uncovered during this retreat look and feel like in your daily life?

Intentional living

Intentional living means to live on purpose, to be present and fully engaged in our lives and to make conscious, aligned choices. It is the difference between moving through our days in a hazy fog of automatic pilot mode and feeling powerless, and being fully engaged and empowered in the life we are living. An intention is an anchor point that you can stay tethered to to ensure you are living in alignment, and are mindful and present.

An intention initiates mindfulness, and slow, soft living. "Purpose" is something a lot of people feel their lives elude. The mistake they make is thinking that a sense of purpose is something found in something else, like a job title, a person or a place, or that it might be found way off in some distant future. But really, purpose is a feeling; it is a state of being and a level of consciousness we bring to all that we do. It can be present for us in every unfolding moment, through intention and conscious choice. To live "on purpose" is to embody intentional living.

You have just transformed the time and space you gifted yourself for this retreat from any old time and space into something sacred and special, simply through intention and conscious choice. You can transform your whole life in this way too.

Reflect: What is your intention moving forward?

Authentic living

You may have chosen a number of exercises and practices that focus on authentic living, such as the "Reconnect to your values" and "What lights you up" journalling exercises in Chapter Three (see Self-reflection exercises). Whether you did or not, the chances are you will have felt a sense of authenticity during your retreat.

It is often said that your authentic self is the one you embody when you return home and shut the door to the world. The version of you that doesn't have to hold up a mask or pretend to be anything other than who you are and what you're feeling at any moment. Your authentic self is the light and the shadow. The more we allow ourselves to be "true" the more respect we have for ourselves. The more we integrate all parts of ourselves the more we are able to love and accept ourselves fully.

I interviewed an incredible woman called Charya Hilton as part of a meditation series a few years ago. She told me "Some people are very silent and quiet and some people are just nuts. You know, like, really crazy, funny, warm. But I think that the quality of someone who I would call enlightened is a person who really loves and accepts themselves". The misconnection with spiritual or mindful living is the perception that it means we must always be "nice" or "good", or that we should deny any feelings that aren't deemed as "evolved". But if we are putting on a front for another person or the world to look mindful, spiritual or evolved we are not living authentically. This kind of disconnect can lead to us losing self-respect and leads us down a path further and further away from our true self. To be authentic means to live by your values. It means to allow yourself joy, peace and alignment.

Reflect: How can you let yourself be more of who you truly are? What would an authentic life look like for you?

Daily rituals

You will have engaged with at least one ritual during your retreat – the opening ceremony – and you may have chosen to explore many more from the ritual section in Chapter Three. A daily ritual after your retreat can also bring a great sense of comfort, and offer you a sense of stability during challenging times.

What differentiates a ritual from a routine is the level of consciousness you bring to it. Anchoring each day with intention and presence through a simple ritual can be a powerful way of empowering yourself, helping you to live intentionally and authentically.

It might take a while to embed a ritual as a daily practice, and you must be conscious not to let a ritual slip into a routine, performed without conscious awareness (although if these two things occur, just know it is completely normal). But simple daily rituals like starting your day with a simple meditation practice, saying affirmations in the bathroom mirror or showing up to a seasonal altar to remind yourself of your current intention are all potent and powerful practices. Show up to your chosen daily rituals consistently for a few months and I am certain you will agree with me. It can be so simple, it can be pleasurable, and it can create magic.

Reflect: What daily rituals would you like to embed moving forward? How can you support yourself to embed these as a conscious, daily ritual practice?

Creativity

Creativity allows for emotional and self-expression. It can assist a healing process, anchor us in a flow state of presence and also aid in the integration process.

We are all creative beings and not one of us has been left out. Creativity isn't always something we can hang in a frame. Every meal you make, every idea you bring to life, every problem you've ever solved is a creative act. Creativity is an energy that turns a blank page into a painting, pain into a poem and life into a masterpiece. And creativity as part of an integration process can engage both the subconscious and the conscious mind, as it can help lead to a sense of wholeness and process emotions and experiences on all levels of our being.

Create: Spend some time at the end of your retreat creatively expressing the experience. This might be through writing a blog or a poem, drawing a picture, creating a nature mandala or dancing. Whatever feels right for you, take a few moments before your retreat draws to a close creatively expressing the experience you have had.

Writing your future self a note practice

This is one of my favourite activities on group and self-led retreats, and it is one of the very final things we do before drawing the retreat to a close.

For this practice, you will write yourself a note, addressing it to, and signing it off from, yourself. Make it a love letter, and a letter of guidance and advice. Let your future self know how you hope they are feeling, what they have changed or what they are currently embodying. Remind them of the insights and lessons you uncovered on your retreat. And remind them of their beauty and worth.

On group led retreats, I ask guests to seal their letters in an envelope and write their postal address on the front. A few months later, I skip and hop my way to the postbox (mailbox) to post them back to them. On your self-led retreat, you might choose to seal your note in an envelope, put a stamp on it and hand it to a trusted friend and ask them to post it back to you at a random moment in the future. Alternatively, seal your letter in an envelope and store it somewhere safe to stumble across at a later date.

Create: Write yourself a love letter. Seal it in an envelope and keep it somewhere safe or ask a friend to post it back to you at a later date.

Crossing a threshold

Just as you took a sacred pause to start your retreat, I'd encourage you to do the same to close your retreat. Group retreats will usually feature a closing circle, which are an opportunity to reflect and share insights on ongoing intentions. This acts as a powerful threshold into the integration stage, where you will begin to embody insights and implement changes in everyday life. This is the power of retreats, where the real magic happens.

Retreat closing ceremony

You have reached the very end of your retreat. I hope there's a big, peaceful smile on your face, and that your heart feels open and your energy feels topped up. I honour you for taking this time for self-leading and prioritising you and your self-care.

Just as you opened your retreat with a simple ceremony, I encourage you to close with something similar to seal off the experience.

You will need:

a sage stick or palo santo stick, or an aura or room cleansing spray (optional); a lighter or matches; your journal and a pen; and a candle.

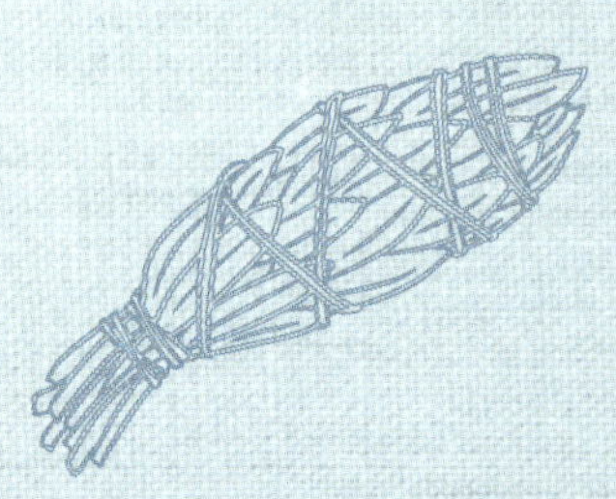

The ceremony

- For this ceremony, you will keep it simple. You might like to cleanse the space you are in one last time with sage or palo santo (if permitted) or an aura or room cleansing spray. You might like to skim-read through your journal, taking note of any learnings, reflections or ah-ha moments that surfaced during your retreat. You may also wish to use your journal to jot down your intentions to carry forward.

- When you are ready to begin, light a candle to symbolise the start of the ceremony.

- Just as you did with your opening ceremony, place both hands over your heart, close your eyes and become aware of your heart space. Spend a few minutes in this short meditation, focusing on your heart space and your breath.

- Conjure up feelings of gratitude, love and hope, and allow a smile to form on your face. Allow these feelings to flood through the body, imagining every cell vibrating with gratitude, love and hope.

- Take a moment to honour yourself for choosing this retreat. Honour the space that has held you. Honour the energy that has moved through you. Honour the earth, the sun, the moon, the stars and the universal energy around you. Allow a sense of place and connection and a deep sense of gratitude for getting to experience it all.

- Say out loud "Thank you, thank you, thank you".

- Take a long, slow deep breath and open the palms of your hands out facing upward in a receptive gesture. Spend a few moments here in a receptive pose, still smiling. Then, open your arms out wide as you take a breath in. Imagine scooping up all the good, positive, strong, wise energy, and allow the palms of your hands to meet, stretched out above your head. Draw that energy down to your heart space, and remind yourself of any intention you wish to carry forward from this retreat.

- Bow your head to your heart, honouring yourself and the experience for one last time, before opening your eyes.

- To signify the end of your ceremony and your retreat, blow the candle out.

Closing thoughts

Soft, slow, creative living is the antidote to the mad race of the modern world. Mindfulness is the gateway. Nature is the tonic. Self-care is the action. And intention and rituals are what can keep us on track.

Going on a retreat reminds us of this, as retreats have the power to be the catalyst for deep and lasting change and healing. But it is how we implement and embody that change in our day-to-day lives that really matters.

When we embark on a self-led retreat, we are initiating the process of embodied self-care, self-leadership and responsibility right from the very start. We take all we have learned and uncovered with us back into daily life. Retreats shouldn't be a luxury, only accessible to a tiny percentage of the population, and they don't have to be. Self-led retreats show us this.

If you have engaged in this experience from start to finish, I am so proud of you! I would genuinely love to hear how you got on. In fact, I actively encourage you to share, if it feels right. Tag me on Instagram (@joeyhulin_writer) in your pictures and reflections from your retreat if you share them on social media once you are back to "normal" life. Your post might inspire someone else to take some time for themselves. Let's start a revolution!

Retreats are such a huge and important part of my life, and I am so grateful for the people, insights, magic and nourishment they have brought me. I never would have thought that they would be such a big part of my life years ago, as it wasn't by design. Instead, I have fallen in love with and built a life involving retreats by following the breadcrumbs laid out along my path, and by using my inner guidance system as a compass. It is a great privilege for me to hold space for others on retreat, and to learn how to do the same for myself on my own self-led retreats.

As I write these words to you now, I am 35 weeks pregnant, bouncing up and down on a huge inflatable yoga ball, rubbing my rather large belly in the pauses between sentences. A whole new, wild adventure lies ahead for me and my baby girl. I know my relationship with work and retreats will undoubtedly change. But I have a feeling my relationship with self-led retreats will only become deeper and more important, especially as a single mum.

As I set my own intentions for motherhood, one thing I know I do want to model to my daughter is what self-care and self-kindness looks like and how important it is. This will be a lifelong journey for me. I hope that by intending to commit to this that she too learns how to love and accept herself, and treat herself like the guest of honour in her own life. And I wish this for you too.

I hope this book has offered you guidance, inspiration and support to prioritise what makes you feel good and what tops you up. I hope it has helped you reconnect to yourself, to the natural world and to the mystical, magical, universal energy that is alive in all things. I hope it felt like there was a hand to hold as you navigated your shadow and I hope that it was the wind in your sails of your journey toward alignment, authenticity and to shining brightly in this world. I hope you feel supported in integrating and embodying all you've learned during your retreat into your daily life. I hope it's reminded you of what you already are: exactly who, what and where you need to be, with a future so bright it's illuminating.

Finally, I hope you return to this book again and again, and choose to "retreat yourself" regularly, whether it's a monthly retreat afternoon in your garden or an annual retreat somewhere immersed in nature. See it as life and soul maintenance.

Quite simply, you deserve it

About the author

Joey Hulin is a meditation teacher, author and poet based in Cornwall. She offers a down-to-earth, warm and playful approach to mindful living and spirituality. The founder of wellness company Horizon Inspired, she offers retreats, online courses and meditations around the world, creating nourishing opportunities for people to pause and reconnect. Joey's first book *Your Spiritual Almanac* was published in September 2021 by Laurence King Publishing, shortly followed by *Mind & Bowl* in 2022. Her third book, *Your Manifesting Year*, was published by Ebury in 2023. *The Meditation Yearbook*, published by David and Charles, followed in 2024.

She is an active teacher on the Insight Timer app and is currently studying for an MA in Transpersonal Psychology.

Acknowledgements

I am writing these acknowledgements as I enter into the fifth week postpartum, while my baby girl sleeps on my chest. I've been immersed in a retreat of a different kind these last five weeks, one where self-care looks like a shower a day, and meditations look like gazing into the eyes of a newborn. Friends have filled my freezer with nutritious meals and my daily movement tends to involve a gentle rocking motion. Connection to nature feels more important now than ever. Deep in this retreat, remembering the power of intention transforms tough moments and deepens the joy. Stolen moments here and there given to feeling such gratitude for this book, soon to be birthed into the world too. Thank you to all at D&C for this opportunity. I truly hope readers – you – feel inspired to retreat yourself! Thank you especially to Lizzie, Chloe, Jess and Jess for being brilliant! Retreats have been such a huge part of my life for almost a decade. The team I get to work alongside, and the guests who attend, are why I keep showing up. A deep heartfelt thank you goes to my retreat colleagues and friends Sian Reid, Izzie Maqueen and the rest of the team at 7th Rise, and Tia Tamblyn and the rest of the Botelet crew. Thank you Sam Cawsey, Robyn Proctor, Lisa Allen and Linda Shabtai for bringing your magic to retreats. And finally to every guest who has shared a retreat experience over the years. What a privilege it has been holding space for people in beautiful spaces.

Index

A VERBENA BOOK

Verbena is an imprint of David and Charles, Ltd, Suite A, Tourism House, Pynes Hill, Exeter, EX2 5WS

First published in the UK and USA in 2025

A catalogue record for this book is available from the British Library.

ISBN-13: 9781446315699 paperback
ISBN-13: 9781446315705 EPUB

This book has been printed on paper from approved suppliers and made from pulp from sustainable sources.

Printed in China through Leo Paper Product Ltd. for: David and Charles, Ltd, Suite A, Tourism House, Pynes Hill, Exeter, EX2 5WS

10 9 8 7 6 5 4 3 2 1

Publishing Director: Ame Verso
Senior Commissioning Editor: Lizzie Kaye
Publishing Manager: Jeni Chown
Editor: Jessica Cropper
Copy Editor: Chloe Murphy
Lead Designer: Sam Staddon
Design: Joelle Wheelwright and Jess Pearson
Pre-press Designer: Susan Reansbury
Production Manager: Beverley Richardson

David and Charles publishes high-quality books on a wide range of subjects. For more information visit www.davidandcharles.com.

Follow us on Instagram by searching for @dandcbooks.

Layout of the digital edition of this book may vary depending on reader hardware and display settings.